101 Art Destinations in the U.S.

101 Art Destinations in the U.S.

WHERE ART LIVES COAST TO COAST

OWEN PHILLIPS

Rizzoli Electa

Contents

South Atlantic

Midwest

South Central

Mountain

Southwest

Pacific C...

Introduction

OWEN PHILLIPS

A temple to culture built by robber barons, a front yard full of scrap wood painted with bible verses, and bulldozer-enabled carve-outs so big they can be seen from space: the United States is packed with art. Everyone who has made America what it is today is represented in this book: from the great Native American nations to the first European colonists, the society painters trained in France, and those who were shut out of the academy and taught themselves how to paint.

Most people who care about art have a handful of local museums they visit regularly. They'll make a point of checking out a new piece of public art they've heard about in the news and visit the big museums when they travel. And then there are people who organize their lives around art. They might be painters, photographers, teachers, collectors, curators, researchers, students, or just a kind of superfan; for these die-hards, I have written this book and brought together more than 100 American sites that matter. I owe it to my parents, Mary and Edward, who make wonderful paintings and even show together. They took my brother and me to museums nonstop (and my bias for the ones I spent the most time in throughout my youth will certainly be clear). I blame my love for Brutalist architecture on the many days spent running around Mario Ciampi's Berkeley Art Museum in the pre-earthquake safety days. My parents also taught me to look for art everywhere—I've never forgotten an overnight train ride through Montana where they challenged us to draw what we saw in the dark outside the sleeping compartment windows.

I obsessively make lists—not to-do lists, but lists of favorite records, the most interesting people I've met, the books I've read. The geeky stuff. So, making this list was fun, but also maddening. There are hundreds of worthy museums, all serving their communities and expanding the arts' reach in their own ways. There are public monuments from all eras that inspire the people who live and work among them. And there are so many odd moments: moving tributes to human creativity that come in unexpected packages.

Take the museums: there are the big city behemoths with world-changing artworks in their halls; the humbler spaces that dig into one area, or even one creator's work, in ways that make them one-of-a-kind and essential visits; and nearly everything in between. Take the sculpture parks: they range from well-manicured formal gardens to shaggier, wild spaces that pit their steel and stone constructions against the elements in more dramatic ways.

My favorite sites are the ones that are inextricable from their geography and their history. They couldn't be anywhere else. Some of these are hard to get to, but traveling through the landscapes that moved the artists themselves enhances the experience. A short list of road trips (Suggested Itineraries, p. 256) is included in the back of the book, intended to inspire your own art tourism.

So could you call this a bucket list for art lovers? The book certainly includes the best-known collections, singular experiences, and key art historic moments you studied in school; but it is also meant to start conversation, provoke debate, inspire new lists, and encourage far-flung trips.

NOTE: This book does not include the many wonderful museums that drive the art world but don't have permanent collections, nor does it include commercial galleries. It does include some sites that take a little effort to get into or are rarely open, but none that are closed to the public. There are a few sites that I very much wanted to include but did not for a variety of reasons and they bear noting here: The Studio Museum in Harlem, a historically important institution that continues to do forward-thinking exhibitions of new and older work, closed temporarily to break ground on a new building just as I began writing this book. It will reopen in 2021 in what promises to be spectacular new digs designed by star architect David Adjaye. The Hood Museum in New Hampshire is also closed for renovation at the time of this writing, so I decided not to include Jose Clemente Orozco's phantasmagoric murals even though it is still possible to drop in. Charles Ross's *Star Axis* is a bizarre architectonic head trip in New Mexico which has been under construction for 40 years but already seems in tune with the ancients. It should open finally in 2020. Though I do write about Michael Heizer's *City*—because its rumblings have already been felt in the art world for many years—it also won't be open until 2020. And after much deliberation, I reluctantly excluded Walter De Maria's *Lightning Field* because so few spots are available to stay overnight there each year. (But I encourage readers to give it a shot nonetheless.)

Northeast

Winslow Homer Studio

PROUTS NECK, MAINE

PORTLAND MUSEUM OF ART
7 CONGRESS SQUARE
PORTLAND, ME 04101

In the living room of this Arts and Crafts house on a rocky peninsula, one window frames a view of the coast. Squint and you can see it: Winslow Homer's signature is scratched in the glass. It might be a stretch to speculate that he meant to sign the view as his own work, but it wouldn't be crazy. Homer had the former stable moved closer to the shore in the 1880s, along with adding the second-floor balcony, regarded as a key inspiration and vantage point for some of his greatest works. He did this after returning from a couple of years of painting working people on the coast of England, a sojourn credited with eliminating the last vestiges of sentimentalism and crowd-pleasing color (meant to comfort viewers after the trauma of the Civil War) from his work and opening the door to his mature style.

Many historic artists' homes are spare in an effort to only display objects of the original owner; Homer's home is spare because he liked it that way. In that same living room, a simple daybed sits under some china plates painted by his mother, Henrietta, and some fish he taxidermied himself.

It's a Zen space, focused on the sea. Art critic Holland Cotter of the *New York Times* called Homer the "first great post-God landscape painter" because, unlike that of the Hudson River School painters, his landscape and its transcendent light wasn't a lesson in divine grace; the booming waves that crashed night and day were violence and danger and reality. That he used his skills from early days as a newspaper illustrator to bring out the drama in a masterpiece like *Undertow*, from 1886 (now at the Clark Art Institute, p. 26), or *The Fog Warning*, from 1885, doesn't make the rocks and sea any less threatening than a great landscape-only painting like *Northeaster*, from 1895.

The Maine coast inspired many artists—John Marin, Arthur Dove, and Marsden Hartley, to name a few. You could travel up and down the coast and see vistas they painted—Mt. Katahdin was a favorite topic of Hartley's, for instance—but at Prouts Neck, specific rock formations from Homer's paintings can still be identified on a walk along the path just below the house; for those who've spent time with his paintings, it can be a moment of profound connection with the artist. Homer inspired so many: N. C. Wyeth (who illustrated an edition of Melville's *Moby-Dick*, among other great works about the power of nature) studied him at the direction of his teacher Howard Pyle, and then passed on the appreciation to his son Andrew, whose Maine fame now eclipses Homer's in the popular imagination. Ernest Hemingway said he drew inspiration from Homer's rugged viewpoint, too.

On a visit to Homer's home, you can see the sign he posted out front to keep lookie-loos away: "Warning Mice and Snakes!" But more importantly, at this front row seat on nature's tremendous power, you can feel the artist's prime directive—the only lesson he really gave: "Look at nature, look independently, and solve your own problems."

The Winslow Homer Studio is operated by the Portland Museum Art, and is only accessible by jitney from the museum. Visits—which take place from April through October, and only on select days of the week—must be planned in advance.

The Portland Museum of Art was founded in a mansion in 1908, but got the shot in the arm that would make it a major institution in 1976 with a donation of 17 Homer paintings. Major expansion and gifts followed, including a collection of 50 American modernist works and, later, a trove of Impressionist and Post-Impressionist paintings from a Whitney heiress. It has major works by Childe Hassam, N. C. Wyeth, and one of America's greatest maritime painters, Fitz Henry Lane. It also has some 900 works by Homer.

Next to Grant Wood's *American Gothic*, *Christina's World* by Wyeth's son Andrew might be the most parodied American painting of all time. The painting of Christina Olson, who was paralyzed from the waist down, pulling herself uphill toward the typical New England saltbox house, is an icon nonetheless—and Maine's most popular painter's masterpiece. The painting itself is in the Museum of Modern Art (p. 56), but visitors to the site on the Cushing Peninsula near Rockland can (and do, daily) reenact Christina's struggle—and they can also tour the house Wyeth used as both subject and studio for decades. (The Langlais Sculpture Preserve, run by Colby College, is also in Cushing; p. 16.)

The next stop is a visit to the Farnsworth Museum, which owns and operates the Olson House. There you'll see much more of Wyeth's work. The museum specializes in American art, with a true love for painters of Maine. The other Wyeths are there— N. C. and Jamie—but so are Marsden Hartley, Fairfield Porter, George Bellows, Will Barnet, the suffragist Ida Proper, marine-art master Fitz Henry Lane, Thomas Moran, Neil Welliver, John Marin, and Constance Cochrane. There are smaller treats throughout the collection, such as the paintings by Emily Muir, the self-taught modernist architect beloved on the island of Stonington.

If you're sick of rocky shores and work that flirts with the boundaries of illustration, the Farnsworth has the second largest collection of Louise Nevelson's art—she grew up in Rockland. You can see her early paintings from the Art Students League in New York, and examples of her mature, black-relief sculptural work, like *Full Moon* from 1980. The museum also has her intense and exquisite jewelry—powerful miniatures of her work with wood.

Colby College Museum of Art

5600 MAYFLOWER HILL DRIVE
WATERVILLE, ME 04901

The painter Alex Katz—the epitome of New York cool, with his emotionally remote portraits cropped like commercial billboards and flattened like Japanese prints—found himself at the school in Skowhegan, Maine, in 1949, and proceeded to spend every summer until the present in a 19th-century farmhouse in Lincolnville. He became very close to Colby College and eventually donated 400 works to what would become his own 10,000-square-foot wing at the school's America-centric museum. There are collages from his first years in the state, and the large group portraits he became known for by the 1970s. In addition to his wife, Ada, who appears to be giving him a death stare half the time, there are many faces from the high-end Manhattan world he lives in, like John Ashbery, Paul Taylor, Robert Creeley, and Kenneth Koch.

The rest of the museum—which stretches out from a glass box that's guarded by Richard Serra's *4-5-6* and lined with a 3-story Sol LeWitt wall drawing (which looks spectacular through the glass at night)—is not too shabby either. Thanks to robust donors, the museum houses the Lunder Collection of American Art—spanning Winslow Homer to Deborah Butterfield to Maya Lin, not to mention 300 etchings by James Abbott McNeill Whistler. Some highlights: Georgia O'Keeffe's *Lake George in Woods* and Marsden Hartley's *City Point, Vinalhaven*.

In addition to the Katz wing, Colby has dug deep on 3 other artists you won't find in such quantity anywhere else. First, there's a large collection of work by John Marin, who was one of the earliest Americans to play with abstraction, and a member of New York's Alfred Stieglitz circle (which included O'Keeffe and Edward Steichen). He has the contradictory

THE MUSEUM
IS A SCHOOL:

THE ARTIST LEARNS
TO COMMUNICATE;

THE PUBLIC LEARNS
TO MAKE CONNECTIONS

COLBY COLLEGE MUSEUM OF ART

distinctions of having captured the rocky, wild coast of Maine better than almost anyone, and having influenced the Abstract Expressionists with his loose handling of oil paint (almost as if it were watercolors) and his willingness to leave canvas bare.

Colby has also collected 300 prints by the painter Terry Winters (created, for the most part, at New York's legendary Universal Limited Art Editions).

The third artist, lesser known outside of Maine but becoming almost as ubiquitous as the Wyeths across the state, is Bernard Langlais, who was so prolific before he died in 1977 that Colby not only houses an enormous amount of his work, it oversees the distribution of pieces to museums and

public sites. Like Katz, the sculptor and woodcarver was associated with the Skowhegan School. He started out working with making Expressionist oil paintings—he had a Fulbright Scholarship to study Edvard Munch's paintings in Oslo in the 1950s—but gave up painting after a few playful experiments with wood while renovating his cottage in Cushing, Maine. These include a 13-foot-tall horse, a caricature of Richard Nixon, and an homage to Christina Olson, whose home nearby inspired Andrew Wyeth.

Colby oversees the Langlais Sculpture Preserve, which just opened to the public at the end of 2017, and the Langlais Art Trail, a distribution of hundreds of his works up and down

the coast of Maine to small museums and public spaces.

OPPOSITE: INSTALLATION VIEW OF THE COLBY COLLEGE MUSEUM OF ART, WATERVILLE, ME.

PHOTO: © TRENTBELLPHOTOGRAPHY.

ABOVE (COURTYARD): RICHARD SERRA, *4-5-6*, 2000, FORGED WEATHERPROOF STEEL, AS SEEN IN THE PAUL J. SCHUPF SCULPTURE COURT. MUSEUM PURCHASE FROM THE JERE ABBOTT ACQUISITIONS FUND, 2000.002. ON INTERIOR WALL OF BUILDING: LUIS CAMNITZER, *THE MUSEUM IS A SCHOOL*, 2011, SITE-SPECIFIC INSTALLATION. GIFT OF SETH A. THAYER JR. '89 AND GREGORY N. TINDER IN HONOR OF THE STAFF AT THE COLBY COLLEGE MUSEUM OF ART, 2013.509.

PHOTO: © BITTERMANN PHOTOGRAPHY

The Harvard Art Museums

FOGG MUSEUM
BUSCH-REISINGER MUSEUM
ARTHUR M. SACKLER MUSEUM
32 QUINCY STREET
CAMBRIDGE, MA 02138

One of the oldest academic institutions has come through with a state-of-the art way to look at, and think about, art. While combining Harvard's 3 art museums under one roof (by way of an extension to its oldest institution, The Fogg), architect Renzo Piano created the 5-story Calderwood Courtyard, where the disparate collections intersect. With 2 floors of colonnades and a third of glass, it feels both timeless and modern, giving glimpses of different art pieces from different eras. Piano called the glass roof his "Light Machine," and has expertly used it to filter natural light to many of the galleries.

The Fogg is known for its deep collections of Renaissance, Baroque, and Dutch Master paintings as well as one of Vincent van Gogh's most famous self-portraits. The second oldest of the 3 museums, the Busch-Reisinger, has been devoted since 1901 to art from German-speaking countries—it's strong on Vienna Secession and German Expressionism, but it also houses contemporary work by Gerhard Richter and Anselm Kiefer, and the one of the largest collections of Joseph Beuys. The Arthur M. Sackler

dates back only to 1985 but has one of the most important collections of Asian art in the U.S., as well as significant pieces from the ancient and Islamic worlds.

The top level houses the Lightbox Gallery, a high-tech lab connected to all these treasures of the past. Its massive digital wall is a showcase for art and technology, letting visitors call up and compare works from any part of the collection. But Lightbox also allows a look at the science that goes into preservation and conservation, and includes the Forbes Pigment Reference Collection, with over 1,000 pigments in floor-to-ceiling cabinets arranged from red to indigo.

One of the great success stories of these labs is on display: Mark Rothko's *Harvard Murals*, originally installed in 1964 in the campus's Holyoke Center—a penthouse dining room that managed to fade the paintings very quickly. Now they're displayed with digital illumination that brings out the original colors without altering the canvas in any way. At 4 o'clock each day, the projectors are shut off and the transition from the new glow of the old colors to the faded version is fascinating—and one visitors know not to miss.

NEARBY: Twelve minutes across Cambridge toward downtown Boston is MIT (77 Massachusetts Avenue)—the preeminent science and tech school. Its "Arts at MIT" is an aggressive public-art program spread around campus, with some appropriately wonky elements. Look for work by Matthew Richie, Sarah Sze, Antony Gormley, Michael Heizer, Anish Kapoor, and Cai Gao-Qiang.

CALDERWOOD COURTYARD, HARVARD ART MUSEUMS, CAMBRIDGE, MA.

PHOTO: PETER VANDERWARKER © PRESIDENT AND FELLOWS OF HARVARD COLLEGE

#4

The Robert Gould Shaw Memorial

24 BEACON STREET
(AT BOSTON COMMON)
BOSTON, MA 02108

Augustus Saint-Gaudens spent 14 years getting this right—a bronze relief sculpture depicting Union General Robert Gould Shaw leading 1,000 African American volunteers right down Beacon Street to fight in the Civil War. The heroism of the general, who would not return, and that of the soldiers—who faced worse fates if caught down South—are both memorialized here.

Saint-Gaudens is the Rome-trained superstar of the Beaux-Arts American Renaissance, in demand for work in Washington and New York. The commission called for a single equestrian statue, but the Shaw family asked that Saint-Gaudens find a way to include the men Shaw led in the memorial. So the idea of a relief sculpture was born. Saint-Gaudens hired models to pose as the soldiers, and the 1897 memorial has been praised as one of the first truly naturalistic depictions of African Americans in academic American art. It's also considered one of the most moving and successful memorials in the country.

NEARBY: Saint-Gaudens's house and studio (139 Saint Gaudens Road, Cornish, NH) is about two and a half hours away and run by the National Park Service. The original plaster cast for the Shaw Memorial is there, on loan from the National Gallery of Art. You can also see a bronze cast of the memorial Henry Adams commissioned for his wife, which he called *The Mystery of the Hereafter and the Peace of God that Passeth Understanding.*

THE ROBERT GOULD SHAW MEMORIAL, BOSTON, MA.

PHOTO: © USER:PIOTRUS / WIKIMEDIA COMMONS / CC-BY-SA-3.0

Museum of Fine Arts, Boston

465 HUNTINGTON AVENUE
BOSTON, MA 02115

John Singer Sargent is the hero here. His painting *The Daughters of Edward Darley Boit* has pride of place in the new Art of Americas Wing, completed by Foster + Partners in 2010. It's one of Sargent's best works—it's been compared to the work of Édouard Manet and the painting *Las Meninas* by Diego Velázquez. In fact, it's the centerpiece of the new wing, which kicks off on the ground floor by mixing art from Central America and Native Americans with early colonial pieces.

Objects from day-to-day life are interspersed with sophisticated decorative items and some of the awkward early paintings of the newcomers. It lets John Singleton Copley's *Paul Revere* portrait sit next to Paul Revere's iconic work, the *Sons of Liberty Bowl*. The American collections have Winslow Homer's *The Fog Warning* and *Driftwood* and the original (unfinished) Gilbert Stuart portrait of George Washington that was a master for the scores of copies spread out across the country. But they also mix in furniture and other objects with a notation saying that many were made by slaves—or other laborers who were considered unworthy of being credited at the time—and that the museum seeks to find some balance there.

It's something the museum does up and down its long halls—contextualize collections rather than divide them rigidly by chronology or medium. Its Greek and Roman wings, second in size in the U.S. only to the Metropolitan Museum's in New York, seek to bring to life what can be an antiseptic experience. Galleries devoted to the ancients' love of wine mix objects meant for drinking with depictions on vases. One of the MFA's most important pieces, the marble *Bust of Homer* from around the 1st century A.D., is in a gallery that gathers art connected to the *Iliad*. This contextualizing is evident in its Krauthammer section, which re-creates the *Wunderkabinett* idea of art and curiosities from all over the world during the Age of Exploration. And it's evident in the Renaissance galleries where another of the museum's major pieces—the relief sculpture *Madonna of the Clouds* by Donatello, a rare example of his work in the U.S.—is set next to Pier Jacopo Alari Bonacolsi's bronze *Bust of Cleopatra*. (The museum has major works by Peter Paul Rubens, El Greco, and Diego Velázquez. And it has Rembrandt's *Artist in his Studio*.)

The Impressionist and Post-Impressionist galleries have works worth a visit alone: Paul Gauguin's masterpiece *Where Do We Come From? What Are We? Where Are We Going?*; Pierre-Auguste Renoir's *Dance at Bougival*; Vincent van Gogh's *Postman Joseph Roulin*; and 37 Monets, including *La Japonaise*. But it also has a gallery devoted to Impressionist paintings of changing urban life, centered around Gustave Caillebotte's *Man at His Bath*.

In another section, the usual monotonous march of modernism is broken up into smaller narratives: Max Beckmann's influence on American painters; Frida Kahlo and her circle; and a kind of face-off between Pablo Picasso and Jackson Pollock. One focuses on artists from Alfred Stieglitz's gallery, 291, including his wife, Georgia O'Keeffe. (Coincidentally, the museum's excellent photography collection was started in 1927 with a gift of 27 photos from Stieglitz.) One of the best of these new galleries considers Hans Hofmann as teacher, and the painters he influenced: Franz Kline, Robert Motherwell, Helen Frankenthaler, David Smith, and Peter Voulkos, to name a few.

The museum excels in non-Western art, as well, with a spectacular collection of bronze and ivory work from the Benin Empire; from modern-day Nigeria; and from the Yoruba people, including work by Olowe of Ise and Agbonbiofe. The mixing and matching and thinking goes on. Another gallery places Louise Bourgeois's *Pillar* next to similar slender columns from Africa and a Giacometti figure. One of the Asian galleries compares Japanese work made after 1800 destined for the Western market, with that made for domestic consumption.

The new galleries have been widely praised for reversing the Frank Gehry effect in museums and putting the art in front of the architecture. An earlier I. M. Pei addition is now all about contemporary art, with work by El Anatsui, Mona Hatoum, Ken Price,

Anish Kapoor, Kara Walker, Josiah McElheny, and Doris Salcedo.

The interior stairs and rotunda of the Neoclassical original building are adorned with John Singer Sargent murals—easy to forget among all the fireworks in the complex.

NEARBY: The mural cycle that John Singer Sargent started late in his life is in the Boston Public Library's McKim Building on Copley Square (700 Boylston Street). It took on all of religion from pagan times to the present day—he spent 30 years on it. (Unfortunately, some of its value judgements are now understood to be problematic, if not anti-Semitic.)

INSTALLATION VIEW OF JOHN SINGER SARGENT, *THE DAUGHTERS OF EDWARD DARLEY BOIT*, 1882, OIL ON CANVAS. GIFT OF MARY LOUISA BOIT, JULIA OVERING BOIT, JANE HUBBARD BOIT, AND FLORENCE D. BOIT IN MEMORY OF THEIR FATHER, EDWARD DARLEY BOIT. 19.124.

PHOTO: © 2018 MUSEUM OF FINE ARTS, BOSTON

Isabella Stewart Gardner Museum

25 EVANS WAY
BOSTON, MA 02115

As beautiful as this faux Venetian Palazzo's intricate interiors are (Moorish, Medieval, Gothic, and Chinese), visitors are inevitably drawn to something it doesn't have: specifically, 2 Rembrandt paintings and a Vermeer, which were cut out of their frames and stolen in a bold, daytime robbery in 1990, by thieves dressed as policemen. The Dutch Room displays the empty frames. The robbers also scored 5 Degas drawings, a Manet, and others. The unsolved crime is one of the biggest art thefts of all time, and the Gardner Museum's way of keeping the wall warm for the works' eventual return is both tribute and true-crime story.

Part of the thrill when visiting grand, historical revival homes and museums is imagining what life was like there. When the site is truly the artist's or collector's home, (such as Frederic Edwin Church's Olana, say, or even William Randolph Hearst's castle), we imagine the salons, the dinner parties, and walking among the beautiful objects in our bathrobes. Other re-creations are less satisfying: The Getty Villa is modeled after Roman homes but was always meant to house J. Paul Getty's collection of antiquities down the hill from his real home.

The Isabella Stewart Gardner Museum is something different. A socialite who attended regular lectures at Harvard after her marriage, Gardner got the inspiration from time spent in Venice at the Palazzo Barbaro, which had become a kind of ex-pat artist hangout where one could find James Abbott McNeill Whistler, John Singer Sargent, and Ralph Curtis. Her collection got off to an auspicious start: Two of her earliest purchases were Rembrandt's *Self-Portrait, Age 23* and Titian's *Europa*. Gardner lived in private quarters on the fourth floor overseeing the installation of her constantly growing collection of paintings, sculptures, and entire interiors imported from Europe.

While we can't imagine the rooms as lived in in a normal household, we can imagine Gardner letting Sargent take over the Gothic Room as a painting studio one year, or dancers and singers performing for friends on balconies and in hallways. The collection, which has managed to securely hold onto its Fra Angelico, Benvenuto Cellini, Sandro Botticelli, and Piero della Francesca paintings, is matched by the incredible craftsmanship of its rooms.

The museum is forbidden from selling or acquiring any objects, ever; but it didn't stop the successful organization from adding a handsome addition by Renzo Piano, connected by glass walkways to the original building, which houses performance halls, space for temporary contemporary exhibitions, and a place for scholars to study Gardner's library of 7,000 rare books.

COURTYARD, ISABELLA STEWART GARDNER MUSEUM, BOSTON, MA.

PHOTO: SEAN DUNGAN

The Clark Art Institute

225 SOUTH STREET
WILLIAMSTOWN, MA 01267

Some would call it Zen. The Clark had had a reputation for being a bit stuffy— all this focus on 19th-century art— but a 2008 reimagining of the entire campus breathed fresh life into a vital collection. Japanese architect Tadao Ando arranged the new buildings for the Clark around a 3-tiered reflecting pool, creating an elegant frame for everything that would be put inside. (Master interior architect Annabelle Selldorf created the gallery spaces.)

Those impressive holdings include French Impressionist, Academic, and American paintings, and were started by Robert Sterling Clark (heir to the Singer Sewing Machine company) and his wife, Francine. They originally sought Old Master paintings but soon switched to collecting Impressionists, going big on Renoir and including Manet and Monet. In the Academic category, they picked up William-Adolphe Bouguereau's *Nymphs and Satyr* and Jean-Léon Gérôme's *The Slave Market*. Once their focus turned to American painters, they added John Singer Sargent, Winslow Homer, and several great landscapes by George Inness. A later bequest created the Manton Collection for British Art and brought in several works by J. M. W. Turner, Thomas Gainsborough, and John Constable.

INSTALLATION VIEW OF EDGAR DEGAS, *LITTLE DANCER AGED 14*, 1879–91 (CAST 1912–21). CLARK ART INSTITUTE. 1955.45.

PHOTO: © JEFF GOLDBERG/ESTO

The Berkshires

WESTERN MASSACHUSETTS

The gentle beauty of the hills and woods in this part of the state has long attracted sophisticated city dwellers in search of bucolic vacation homes. It's no different for artists and their patrons. Three major house museums and a college museum are worth a trip. (Information about another worthy museum in the area, the Clark Art Institute, can be found on p. 26)

THE FRELINGHUYSEN MORRIS HOUSE AND STUDIO (92 HAW-THORNE STREET, LENOX, MA 01240)

A surprise flash of white and International Style in the woods, the home and studio of Suzy Frelinghuysen and George Morris is a window into a particular moment in American art. The well-connected couple had traveled in Europe and hung out with everyone from Léger to Mondrian, the Arps to the Delaunays. They bought art from Picasso, Matisse, Gris, and Miró. And they brought a passion for abstraction in art and the ideals of objectivity and universalism back to America, which had not yet taken hold.

The studio, built first, was inspired by Le Corbusier but designed by their Yale buddy George Sanderson. The house was partly funded by the sale of Picasso's *The Poet* to Peggy Guggenheim and is filled with Cubist frescoes made by the couple as well as art from their collection, hung today just as they lived with it. Design lovers can spot prewar furniture by Alvar Aalto, Bruno Mathsson, and Gilbert Rohde. Morris pushed modernism in publications, but his best advertisement for it may have been this environmental case study. The site is open only in summer and makes a refreshing stop among the other grand estates around the Berkshires.

CHESTERWOOD (3 WILLIAMSVILLE ROAD, STOCKBRIDGE, MA 01626)

The Georgian Revival home of one of the most successful American sculptors of the nineteenth century, Daniel Chester French, this grand estate's highlight is a large maquette of his Lincoln Memorial in a beautiful studio. The 130-acre grounds also have casts of some of his most famous works such as *The Concord Minuteman* and *The Continents* from the U.S. Custom House in Manhattan.

THE NORMAN ROCKWELL MUSEUM (9 GLENDALE ROAD, STOCKBRIDGE, MA 01261)

This is a temple to illustration, which doesn't always get its due in a museum setting. It houses the *Saturday Evening Post* artist's archives, including 998 paintings by Rockwell. On the grounds are his studio (moved to the property from town), including his easel and props. Its collection includes an array of etchings by New York figurative artist Isabel Bishop; anatomy master George Bridgman; James Montgomery Flagg of Uncle Sam fame; proto-Pop Art advertising master Joe de Mers; Gibson Girl inventor, Charles Dana Gibson; and beloved *New Yorker* artist William Steig.

WILLIAMS COLLEGE MUSEUM OF ART (15 LAWRENCE HALL DRIVE, WILLIAMSTOWN, MA 01267)

Started in a 1926 octagonal brick building that got a 1980s Charles Moore expansion, this museum spans Egyptian art to contemporary work. It has the largest collection of the Post-Impressionist brothers Maurice and Charles Prendergast, as well as *Death on the Ridge Road* by Grant Wood, *Morning in a City* by Edward Hopper, early drawings by Andy Warhol, Tony Oursler's uncanny projected heads, and a set of eyeball benches by Louise Bourgeois that you can sit on.

NORMAN ROCKWELL'S STUDIO ON THE GROUNDS OF THE NORMAN ROCKWELL MUSEUM, STOCKBRIDGE, MA.

PHOTO: COURTESY NORMAN ROCKWELL MUSEUM. ARTWORK COURTESY THE NORMAN ROCKWELL FAMILY AGENCY

Wadsworth Atheneum Museum of Art

600 MAIN STREET
HARTFORD, CT 06103

The Wadsworth is a major American museum that may be lesser known because of the Latin addendum to its name, which speaks to its founder Daniel Wadsworth's desire to create a center for learning. Its iconic, castle-like building gives a hint to its age: Opened in 1844, it's the oldest continuously operating museum in the United States. Wadsworth kicked off the collection in the beginning with paintings by John Turnbull, John Singleton Copley, and the Peale family. But the museum never rested on its laurels; it acquired the best collection of Hudson River School paintings anywhere, including Thomas Cole's *Mount Etna from Taormina* and Frederic Edwin Church's *Hooker and Company Journeying through the Wilderness from Plymouth to Hartford in 1636.*

The Wadsworth expanded throughout the early 20th century with gifts from Samuel Colt's widow and J. P. Morgan that resulted in adding Tudor and Renaissance Revival buildings. Morgan's gift included the bulk of his collections in antiquities.

Continuing the architectural Disneyland factor, the museum also boasts one of the first International Style interiors in the U.S., in the upstairs of the otherwise Neo-Palladian Goodwin House.

The museum is known for many firsts: It's the first American institution to collect Caravaggio, Anthony van Dyck, Francisco de Zurbarán, Paul Gauguin, Joan Miró, Balthus, and Salvador Dalí. It staged the first American show on Surrealism and the country's first ever Pablo Picasso retrospective, in 1934.

In 2015, a major renovation was completed, rehanging all of the permanent collection. It's regarded as one of the most successful reconceivings

of a museum ever, and its highlight is the double-height Grand Hall of the Morgan Memorial building—hung to mimic the collection's 1749 painting by Giovanni Paolo Panini, *Interior of a Picture Gallery with the Collection of Cardinal Silvio Valenti Gonzaga*, with paintings everywhere.

Critics note the new layout's power throughout to mix less famous works with blockbuster pieces like Caravaggio's *Saint Francis of Assisi in Ecstasy*, or even major postwar abstraction pieces by Jackson Pollock, Mark Rothko, and Barnett Newman, or contemporary superstars like Kara Walker, Cindy Sherman, and Bill Viola.

The most popular painting, according to staff, is a fusion of the collection's decorative-arts collections and obsession with European painting: Pre-Raphaelite William Holman Hunt's incredibly complex and gorgeous *The Lady of Shalott* from the late 1890s.

NEARBY: In 1978, the city of Hartford commissioned Minimalist sculptor Carl Andre to create a public pier near City Hall (on the corner of Main Street and Gold Street, around the corner from the Wadsworth). Andre was at the peak of his fame for his steel-plate floor pieces (you can see them at Dia:Beacon, p. 42), but for Hartford, he gathered 36 local rocks, arranged them in a triangle, and called it a day. The piece, titled *Stone Field Sculpture*, became a lightning rod in the city: easy to ridicule, easy to deface. Ultimately, local artists and the leadership of the Atheneum stood up to the desecration and started to stoke a certain fondness in town for "the Rocks," as they became known.

Yale University Art Gallery

1111 CHAPEL STREET
NEW HAVEN, CT 06510

YALE CENTER FOR BRITISH ART
1080 CHAPEL STREET
NEW HAVEN, CT 06510

As many people come to see Louis Kahn's building for the Yale University Art Gallery as they do the art. The architect's first commission was also Yale's first modernist building—and its glass, steel, and concrete make everything in the collection look stunning.

Opened in 1832 with a collection of Revolutionary War paintings by John Trumbull, the gallery was housed in Neoclassical, Neo-Gothic, and Renaissance Revival buildings before Kahn's addition.

The Neoclassical building is now gone, and the Gothic building has been restored to show the American collection, with everyone from Benjamin West to Gerald Murphy represented in grand spaces awash in natural light. The encyclopedic museum has strong departments across the continents—and spectacular displays of ancient art, much of which came from Yale's own archaeological excavations in the Near East.

But the paintings are what attract the most attention, including highlights like van Gogh's *The Night Café*. The modern painting collections have, at their core, works by the Société Anonyme—a group founded by Katherine S. Dreier, Marcel Duchamp, and Man Ray—given to Yale in 1941. They include work by Constantin Brancusi, El Lissitzky, and Piet Mondrian. Other greats are Joseph Stella's *Brooklyn Bridge*, Jackson Pollock's *Number 13A: Arabesque*, and Roy Lichtenstein's *Blam*.

Two of Man Ray's "rayographs" from 1941 were the first photos to enter the collection, and the photography collection expanded widely in 1971 with work by then Yale professor Walker Evans. (It now holds complete sets of photos by Robert

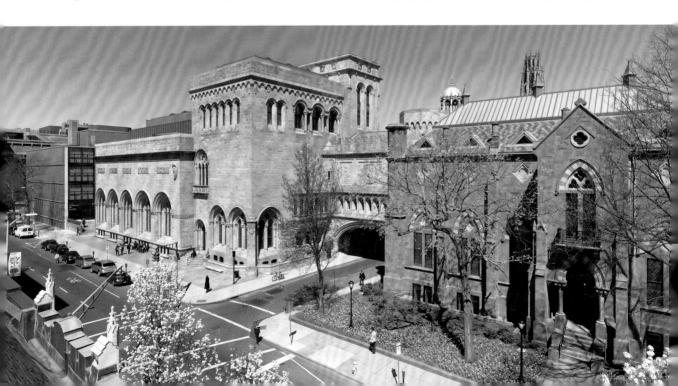

Adams and Lee Friedlander—and work by the art stars the Yale photography school churns out).

Across the street is the Yale Center for British Art in another glass-and-steel masterpiece—Kahn's final building, opened in 1977, after his death. After a refurbishment in 2016, it's really one of the best-looking sets of art galleries anywhere—with perfect pacing and beautiful light to complement grand paintings like George Stubbs's *Horse Attacked by Lion* and work by Turner, Constable, and Reynolds. The collection was a gift from Yale graduate Paul Mellon, and is the largest collection of British art outside of England, spanning medieval times to the present. Modern work includes major pieces by Francis Bacon, Lucian Freud, Ben Nicholson, Henry Moore, Barbara Hepworth, Wyndham Lewis, Maggi Hambling, and Yinka Shonibare MBE.

NEARBY: On the Yale campus sits Maya Lin's *Women's Table*—a pedestal with running water over it that both celebrates the first women to become students at Yale and laments the years they weren't allowed. You can also find Claes Oldenburg's *Lipstick (Ascending) on Caterpillar Tracks*—an antiwar piece from 1969 that was done in collaboration with Yale students, and remains one of the trickster sculptor's best works.

OPPOSITE: YALE UNIVERSITY ART GALLERY, WITH VIEW OF **(LEFT TO RIGHT)** THE LOUIS KAHN BUILDING, OLD YALE ART GALLERY BUILDING, AND STREET HALL, NEW HAVEN, CT.

PHOTO: CHRISTOPHER GARDNER/YALE UNIVERSITY ART GALLERY

ABOVE: INSTALLATION VIEW OF THE ANCIENT ART GALLERIES, YALE UNIVERSITY ART GALLERY, NEW HAVEN, CT.

PHOTO: JESSICA SMOLINSKY/YALE UNIVERSITY ART GALLERY

Mid-
Atlantic

George Eastman Museum

900 EAST AVENUE
ROCHESTER, NY 14607

There are a lot of young photo museums out there, and, of course, MoMA and the Metropolitan Museum in New York City are the kings: They have collections that defined photography as an art form. But no museum quite tells the story of photography from its invention to its earliest artistic achievements and its eventual celebration as an art form as the George Eastman Museum. It's the oldest photo museum in the world (and one of the oldest movie archives), and it's all on the impressive estate of Kodak's founder.

That the collections trace the development of technology alongside the maturation of a medium makes it fascinating: The collections include beautiful cameras of the past, and examples of nearly every process and printing method ever devised—including the largest group of daguerreotypes in the world. Its first collections were of medical photography made during the Civil War, and it has a top collection of landscape work from the American West, from Carleton Watkins to Ansel Adams. It has a major collection of the glass negatives of French photojournalist Charles Chusseau-Flaviens, who worked from the 1890s to the 1910s. It has the photographic estates of

Lewis Hine and Edward Steichen, as well as major work by Andy Warhol. One item not to miss is Napoleon Sarony's portrait of Sarah Bernhardt from 1880.

It's not just a fussy old place: In 1975, it staged the show *New Topographics*, featuring Robert Adams, Lewis Baltz, Stephen Shore, Bernd and Hilla Becher, and others, and it changed the photo world in America and Europe forever. (A good part of the photo space Pier 24, in San Francisco, is devoted to this show; p. 221.) Still relevant, the Eastman collects contemporary photographers such as Sebastião Salgado, Cindy Sherman, Adam Fuss, Vik Muniz, and Mickalene Thomas. Even when it examines the past, it does so in exciting ways: A recent show was devoted to flammable nitrate film and involved color blowups showing decay and discoloration—it was at once scientifically and aesthetically fascinating.

NEARBY: The Memorial Art Gallery (500 University Avenue) at the University of Rochester is known especially for its devotion to Wendell Castle, the man who blurred the realms of art and furniture. It was the first museum to acquire his work, which plays with expectations in elegantly surreal ways. MAG has 13 major pieces by Castle (who died in 2018), including the massive *Library Sculpture*, the early *Blanket Chest*, and comical and self-explanatory beauties, *Squid Chair*, *Cloud Shelf*, and *Chair Standing on Its Head*. Out front is a set

of cast-iron street furniture, complete with a lamp, called *Unicorn Family*.

There are treasures in the African, Egyptian, and Ancient sections, and paintings by an array of Old Masters and master modernists such as Thomas Hart Benton's *Boomtown*, Hans Hoffmann's *Ruby Gold*, and Stuart Davis's *Landscape with Garage Lights*. In the Fountain Court, you'll find Luca Giordano's monumental altarpiece *The Entombment* near a Baroque organ from Florence—the only full-size Italian organ in the U.S. Even when not being used for concerts, the swoops and curves surrounding its pipes are a fitting complement to Castle's imaginative woodwork.

INSTALLATION VIEW OF *DREAMING IN COLOR: THE DAVIDE TURCONI COLLECTION OF EARLY CINEMA*, GEORGE EASTMAN MUSEUM, ROCHESTER, NY.

PHOTO: COURTESY GEORGE EASTMAN MUSEUM, 2018

Albright-Knox Art Gallery

1285 ELMWOOD AVENUE
BUFFALO, NY 14222

The collection at Albright-Knox started in 1862 when Albert Bierstadt donated his 3-year-old painting *The Marina Piccola, Capri*. It kicked off a museum that, despite its Neoclassical temple building, prided itself on always collecting contemporary art, from to when Impressionists were contemporary Cubists and modernists of all stripes. To up the ante, in 1939, it created the Contemporary Room, which showed whatever was cutting-edge—even if the directors weren't sure it was museum-worthy yet. That room led to early acquisitions of work by Amedeo Modigliani, Chaim Soutine, and Henry Moore over the years.

The museum has Edgar Degas and Mary Cassatt and Vincent van Gogh and Henri Matisse and Pablo Picasso. Frida Kahlo's *Self-Portrait with Monkey* shouldn't be missed. It also has tremendous holdings in postwar and1970s art, including Willem de Kooning, Joan Mitchell, Bridget Riley, Mark Rothko, and Robert Rauschenberg. It has the most Clyfford Still paintings—31 of them—outside of his museum in Denver (p. 189). And it has the complete archives of the folk art–influenced sculptor Marisol.

The museum has not slouched in the 21st century. It still plows ahead with additions to the collection by Matthew Barney, Mark Bradford, Theaster Gates, Subodh Gupta, and Kara Walker. And it has hired Rem Koolhaas's firm OMA to build a new addition to open sometime in the 2020s. (The modern addition by Gordon Bunshaft from 1962 is already full.)

Outdoors you'll find Alexander Liberman, Beverly Pepper, and Tony Smith, along with younger artists like Do Ho Suh, Liam Gillick, and Jason Middlebrook.

NEARBY: The Burchfield Penney Art Center (1300 Elmwood Avenue), part of Buffalo State College, is just blocks away, and has the world's largest collection of the American watercolorist Charles E. Burchfield. The underrated visionary, who was a friend of Edward Hopper, painted nature and his native small-town Ohio with manic, throbbing energy that seemed to intimate knowledge of inner lives of inanimate objects of all kinds. Art critic Jerry Saltz praises the purity of Burchfield's vision by saying everyone from Vincent van Gogh to Caspar David Friedrich to Marsden Hartley seems to have influenced him. Burchfield's influence continues to this day as we see hallucinatory landscapes from many artists.

EXTERIOR VIEW OF ALBRIGHT-KNOX ART GALLERY WITH ALEXANDER LIBERMAN, *BOND*, 1969, PAINTED STEEL, OVERALL: 91 × 101 × 222 IN. COLLECTION ALBRIGHT-KNOX GALLERY, BUFFALO, NEW YORK; GIFT OF SEYMOUR H. KNOX, JR., 1969 (K1969:32). © THE ALEXANDER LIBERMAN TRUST.

PHOTO: TOM LOONAN

Olana State Historic Site

5720 STATE ROUTE 9G
HUDSON, NY 12534

Some people are enthralled by Hudson River School paintings—those lush mid-19th-century artworks that romanticize the vastness of the American landscape—and some walk right by them. It's easy to write off their overblown atmospheric effects—God's light shining through the clouds and such—and it can be hard in the photo and video age to tap into the mind-set of people for whom the unspoiled, wild landscape stood in for so many ideals.

A visit to Olana can cure that skepticism. Perched on 126 acres above the river just outside of the town of Hudson, the view across to the Catskill Mountains is literally where the line "Purple mountain's majesty" came from. Frederic Edwin Church, one of the leading painters of the movement, built this Victorian mansion, with its Middle Eastern flights of decorative fancy, in the 1870s—after already becoming an art star—and worked here until he died in 1900. To picture him here, living with the landscape day in and day out, is to get inside the painting—even though his most famous were of South America or imagined ancient Greek and Roman ruins.

Inspired by a trip to Damascus, Beirut, and Jerusalem, Church worked with architect Calvert Vaux—who was simultaneously at work on all the buildings and bridges in New York City's Central Park—to insert what he had seen into seemingly every surface of the new house. Even the window frames are a glorious mishmash of shapes from abroad. He bought the land a decade earlier, familiar with the area from having visited his teacher, another major Hudson River School painter, Thomas Cole, who lived across the river in Catskill.

Tours of the home go through all the rooms, and a vision of Victorian day-to-day life forms and enchants. The Middle Eastern motifs enliven even the most utilitarian of hallways, and the Persian windows of the open-air bell tower frame the river view. During his travels, Church went by camel to Petra, in Lebanon, a dangerous journey in those days, and Olana's sitting-room walls are covered in sketches and paintings of the pink sandstone cliffs there.

There are several major paintings by Church on view, and there is a photo of Mark Twain when he came to visit. Olana also puts on temporary exhibitions and installations, many historical and some with contemporary artists, such as a recent installation in front of the house by Teresita Fernández, and the temporary insertion of a Chuck Close painting into the living room.

NEARBY: The town of Hudson is known for luring out-priced artists from Brooklyn, and its handful of galleries and midcentury-design-focused furniture shops are worth an afternoon. But 3 sites nearby elevate the Sunday afternoon meandering: Basilica Hudson (110 S. Front Street), down by the river in an aptly named 19th-century factory, holds innovative performance-art events. Art Omi (1405 County Route 22, Ghent), 10 minutes away, is a sculpture park with an annual summer arts residency that throws a great show and party. And New York gallerist Jack Shainman runs the School (25 Broad Street, Kinderhook)—a museum-like space that's featured Nick Cave, El Anatsui, Brad Kahlhamer, and more.

DINING ROOM, OLANA STATE HISTORIC SITE, HUDSON, NY.

PHOTO: © 2018 ANDYWAINWRIGHT.COM

Dia:Beacon

3 BEEKMAN STREET
BEACON, NY 12508

A perfect place: Art and industry have never looked better together than at this former Nabisco printing facility in a classic old Hudson Valley factory town. The sawtooth roof, used to light the old factory floor, brings abundant northern light to the Dia Foundation's collection of large art. The focus is on Post-Minimalist work of the 1960s and 1970s, and all that steel—whether John Chamberlain's mashed-up, paint-chipped auto-body sculptures, Carl Andre's polished floor plates, or Richard Serra's monumental patinaed spirals—looks so right in this space. The artist Robert Irwin, known for working with light and sightlines in ways the viewer barely knows he intervened, worked with the Dia to calibrate the whole experience, especially the lighting. (A reprisal of his *Excursus: Homage to the Square*[3] is here, as well—an enchanting maze of scrims that were first shown on a massive scale at Dia's original space in Manhattan's Chelsea district.)

Thanks to Irwin, Agnes Martin—whose canvases of grids done in pencil are stealthy, emotional powerhouses—finally gets true natural lighting and space, apart from her distracting peers, which few museums get right. Dan Flavin's long untitled piece from 1970 gets a nearly football-field-length hall so viewers can contemplate the neon tubes interacting with each other and their reflections. Work that's about space itself can breathe in here: Fred Sandback's yarn installations and Ellsworth Kelly's walls full of carefully laid out geometric grids. Bruce Nauman's video and neon light pieces depend on their position from the viewer, as well—and the building's slightly spooky basement level provides an ideal setting for them.

It's all because the Dia Foundation, created in 1974 by oil heiress Philippa de Menil, has stuck with a singular vision. Its goal was to support work that didn't fit in the refined gallery spaces of its time, and it commissioned, sponsored, or otherwise supported many seminal works of Land Art and other types of installation art, including Walter De Maria's *Earth Room* in SoHo (p. 64), Joseph Beuys's *7000 Oaks* in Chelsea, and bigger projects far away, such as De Maria's *The Lightning Field* in New Mexico. It even acquired Robert Smithson's giant *Spiral Jetty* in Utah in 2010 working hard to preserve it (p. 190), and, in 2018, his wife Nancy Holt's *Sun Tunnels* (p. 193), also in Utah. Its Andy Warhol collection (many displayed at Beacon) helped found the Andy Warhol Museum in Pittsburgh (p. 79).

But you don't need to know or care about this history or these fields of art to be inspired by a visit to Dia:Beacon. Children and anti-Minimalists alike will admit to liking—even understanding—this often-forbidding work, once they see it so beautifully presented.

NEARBY: Down Highway 9 in Cold Spring is Magazzino Italian Art (2700 U.S. 9), a private exhibition space in a sleek modern slab with incredible Hudson River views. Celebrating Arte Povera, the '60s art movement that took a political stance by using grungy, mundane materials, the collection rotates pieces by Alberto Burri, Alighiero Boetti, Lucio Fontana, and other leaders. Open by appointment.

ROBERT IRWIN, *EXCURSUS: HOMAGE TO THE SQUARE*[3], 1998/2015. © ROBERT IRWIN/ARTISTS RIGHTS SOCIETY (ARS), NEW YORK.

PHOTO: © PHILLIP SCHOLZ RITTERMANN, COURTESY DIA ART FOUNDATION, NEW YORK

Storm King Art Center

1 MUSEUM ROAD
NEW WINDSOR, NY 12553

When the owners of the Star Expansion Company—makers of steel fasteners—conceived of their museum, they hoped to build a collection of Hudson River School paintings. But within 5 years of opening the building and adding more acreage, they found they'd bought 13 David Smith sculptures—very stern, abstract bronzes and steel assemblages—and a new direction was underway.

Eventually the place grew to 500 acres, and 2,500 acres were donated to New York State to preserve the views that are framed by some of the biggest sculptures—a giant, orange Mark di Suvero; a set of Alexander Libermans inspired by Chartres Cathedral; a 212-foot Robert Grosvenor built to match the curve of the Schunnemunk Mountain ridge beyond. The landscape, left largely natural with native plants, provides settings for work of many different scales—some dominating knolls, some tucked just off paths in the woods.

Storm King Art Center has collected important pieces but also worked with artists on site-specific installations. Andy Goldsworthy, known for his work that channels the rolling, woodsy landscapes of his native England, built a 750-foot-long stone wall from the remains of an old farm wall. It's his biggest work ever and winds in and around the trees, disappears into a pond, and reappears on the other side for a final run right into the New York State Thruway. Isamu Noguchi embedded a 40-ton stone at the top of a hill, creating a space meant to be played in. And Maya Lin built *Wave Field*, in which 11 acres of grass covering a former gravel pit seem to roll like ocean waves. (She has said she was inspired by Native American mounds around her hometown in Ohio, Japanese culture, and 1970s Land Art.) Other standout pieces are by Forrest Myers, Arnaldo Pomodoro, Louise Bourgeois, Anthony Caro, Ursula von Rydingsvard, Kenneth Snelson, Richard Serra, and Menashe Kadishman.

Storm King is closed for a good part of the winter, so check the website to plan ahead.

NEARBY: Back down the New York State Thruway toward New York City is Edward Hopper's home and studio in Nyack (82 North Broadway). Once a bustling, ship-building place on the Hudson River, Nyack was a perfect laboratory for Hopper's quiet spaces and rooms full of light, and the sense of waiting. His house, which he continued to visit after settling into an apartment in Greenwich Village for life (p. 63), was rescued from demolition in the 1960s and opened as a community art center and tribute to Hopper in 1971. It has a collection of juvenile paintings showing skill and an interest in boats and water that would later reemerge after visits to Monhegan Island in Maine, as well as ephemera, like Christmas cards he made for his family. The house also presents strong temporary exhibitions, such as a recent solo show by up-and-coming painter Mercedes Helnwein and the winner of the first New York State–sponsored Edward Hopper Citation for Visual Artists, Carrie Mae Weems.

Around town you can see the butcher shop that inspired *Seven A.M.* (now in the Whitney Museum, p. 60); the site of the family's dry-goods store where Hopper worked as a teen; and Hopper's gravesite. (The house will provide a map.) Halfway between Nyack and Storm King on Route 9W, in Haverstraw, you'll find the house he painted in *House by the Railroad* in 1930—it was Hopper's painting of this house that Alfred Hitchcock used as a model for the one in *Psycho*, and Terrence Malick used for *Days of Heaven*.

16

Solomon R. Guggenheim Museum

1071 5TH AVENUE
NEW YORK, NY 10128

It seems like the spiral is all that matters. Frank Lloyd Wright's round and upside down ziggurat, which opened in 1959 to great controversy, sports a sloping path that slowly curls to the top. For decades, it has overwhelmed the art within—and most of the million people a year who visit say they came to see the building, not the art.

Originally called the Museum for Non-Objective Painting, it was conceived to house and be a testament to collector Solomon R. Guggenheim's love of abstract art. The mining company heir began collecting Old Masters, but after visiting Wassily Kandinsky's studio in Dessau, Germany, with the artist Hilla von Rebay, he saw the spiritual dimensions of abstract art and dug in: He bought up work by László Moholy-Nagy and Rudolf Bauer, as well as less non-objective but still modernist work by Marc Chagall and Fernand Léger. Rebay became his regular art advisor, and later the director of the museum.

Over the years, other collections were added, broadening the holdings to cover European painting from the Impressionists to the Cubists, and, thanks largely to Solomon's rambunctious cousin Peggy, the Dadaists and Surrealists. It added one of the best collections of '60s and '70s American art in the early 1990s. The collection is a perfect timeline of modernism, and is the core that supports Guggenheim Foundation branches around the world.

Wright's museum blew up the conception of what a museum should be and how art needed to be seen, and it kicked off decades of wilder and wilder museum design. It repeated the feat when it opened a titanium-clad Frank Gehry–designed museum in Bilbao, Spain, which in turn started a boom of small cities building wilder and wilder designs by the likes of Zaha Hadid, Santiago Calatrava, and Herzog & de Meuron. In 2017, the Guggenheim opened a branch in Abu Dhabi designed by Jean Nouvel.

The spiral at the heart of the original building is always problematic, both physically and aesthetically. Wright had to get builders with experience with parking garages and freeways to put it together, and it still always leaked. For artists and curators, there's a sense of challenge reacting to the void at the center of the spiral—some have worked well with the space, such as Jenny Holzer, Dan Flavin, and, most recently, Daniel Buren, who bisected it with a massive, mirrored structure of his own; and some have just filled the space like a mall atrium or airport terminal. Performance artists, on the other hand, have often thrived with the dramatic space; everyone from Philip Glass to Marina Abramovic to Francesco Vezzoli have created work for it.

The collection itself is relegated to decidedly rectangular galleries off the core. Perhaps it's for the better: Even during relatively staid shows, rubbernecking crowds can't help but keep one eye out over the railing. The spiral always wins.

The museum is so elegant and grand it seems of a piece with the older Museum Mile spots along 5th Avenue—but it was only opened in 2001. It's temporary shows continue to dig and shine light on this heady era.

EXTERIOR VIEW OF THE SOLOMON R. GUGGENHEIM MUSEUM, NEW YORK, NY.

PHOTO: NIKREATES / ALAMY STOCK PHOTO

THE THANNHAUSER COLLECTION   THE SOLOMON D GUGGENHEIM MUSEUM

17

The Metropolitan Museum of Art

1000 5TH AVENUE
NEW YORK, NY 10028

THE MET BREUER
945 MADISON AVENUE
NEW YORK, NY 10021

THE MET CLOISTERS
99 MARGARET CORBIN DRIVE
FORT TRYON PARK
NEW YORK, NY 10040

The Metropolitan Museum of Art is the obvious first stop for anyone embarking on an art tour of the United States. It manages to not feel like one of the biggest, most visited museums in the world. It's not the oldest in America—it was founded in 1870, so the Wadsworth Atheneum has it beat by about 30 years—but it is the ur-museum of our imaginations. The entry hall, designed by Robert Morris Hunt and completed in 1902, is simultaneously like a temple and a train station. The thrill doesn't go away even for New Yorkers who go to the Met regularly. The hall can be exploding with tourists, but the museum absorbs them painlessly into multiple entries—up the grand staircase and into the McKim, Mead & White–designed main wings; through the elegant Greco-Roman halls, plunged into the medieval collection with its 3-story-tall iron choir screen from the 18th-century Spanish Cathedral of Valladolid, or face-to-face with mummies in the Egyptian wing.

The sense of being able to wander, stumbling upon new or forgotten treasures as you head toward what you think you came to see, is why the magic works. In that Egyptian wing is an entire sandstone temple, built in 15 B.C. and dedicated to Isis and Osiris, transported and reconstructed block-by-block with hieroglyphs (and 19th-century European graffiti) in 1965. Its position astride a vast reflecting pool, in a soaring glass atrium overlooking the park, gives it a palpable feeling of majesty. But the halls in and out of this wing contain surprisingly moving examples of work from Sumerian, Hittite, Assyrian, and Babylonian cultures, as well.

Down the vaulted halls of the Greek and Roman collections, you'll need to see the Amathus sarcophagus from 5th-century B.C. Cyprus and a bedroom excavated from a Pompeii-adjacent villa as it was before the eruption of Vesuvius in 79 A.D., complete with wraparound frescoes. Veering west, powerful totem poles and enormous carved-wood fishing boats frame a collection from Pacific Northwest tribes. Upstairs is one of the best collections of Impressionism and Post-Impressionism in the Western Hemisphere, and it includes *The Dance Class* by Edgar Degas, *Circus Sideshow* by Georges Seurat, and Paul Gauguin's *Hail Mary*. And just down the hall, the Arms and Armor Room that dominates so many children's memories stands up as art. Adventures like this call to mind the museum's appearance in popular culture—especially the 1967 book by E. L. Konigsburg, *From the Mixed-Up*

Files of Mrs. Basil E. Frankweiler, in which a brother and sister run away to live secretly at the Met.

It never stops: The Charles Engelhard Court displays a loggia by Louis Comfort Tiffany; major work by Augustus Saint-Gaudens, Paul Manship, and Daniel Chester French; and the entire facade of a turn-of-the-20th-century Wall Street bank by Martin E. Thompson. Decorative arts are covered in a maze of period rooms—from Louis XIV to International Style. Keep going and you'll find your way to an unexpectedly serene spot: a Ming dynasty garden court modeled after one in Suzhou.

One of the world's largest collections of Islamic art is at the Met—a fact that wasn't well known until 2011, when a consolidated set of galleries were opened for the first time. The must-sees here are the miniature paintings from Iran and Mughal India—stunning in their color and vitality. Asian art is represented by extensive Chinese calligraphy collections and sculptures representing every major culture and religion on the continent. It's the biggest collection of Asian art in the United States.

The Met was late to collecting African and Oceanic art, as well as art from the Americas, having only looked to these fields after a major gift from Nelson A. Rockefeller in 1969. But it now has everything from Papua New Guinea prayer poles to 40,000-year-old indigenous rock paintings from Australia. Among the most important pieces to see in this collection is the 16th-century, carved-ivory mask of Idia, Queen of the powerful, culturally prolific Benin Empire and the Edo people in Nigeria.

The meat for many is the European Painting galleries, a collection that puts the Met on the list of the top 10 museums worldwide. Major works by nearly every Old Master are here: Giovanni Battista Tiepolo, Peter Paul Rubens, Caravaggio, Titian, Diego Velázquez. Every museum wants a Rembrandt, but the Met has his *Night Watch* and a 1660 *Self-Portrait* that is among his best; like an old friend, it rewards repeated visits.

Some of the most iconic American paintings are here, too, naturally, given that Frederic Edwin Church was one of the original trustees. You can find John Singleton Copley, Thomas Cole, Winslow Homer, Thomas Eakins, and Gilbert Stuart. John Singer Sargent's *Madame X* continues to stun in person, and though it has become a goofy cliché, Emanuel Leutze's *Washington Crossing the Delaware* still gives a thrill. A recent addition is Thomas Hart Benton's *America Today* mural, which for many years hung in a hall between Rockefeller Center and AXA's atrium art collection (p. 58).

The modern wing has masterpieces that can't be missed: Pablo Picasso's *Gertrude Stein*, Jackson Pollock's *Autumn Rhythm*, and Max Beckmann's triptych *The Beginning*, just to name a few. One of the most news-making things the Met does is the basement-level Costume Institute, directed by Anna Wintour of *Vogue* fame, which puts on annual shows that create some of the biggest lines the museum sees.

The photo collection doesn't have the wall space to display everything all the time, but it's as prestigious as can be imagined—it was kicked off by donations from Alfred Stieglitz himself, the man whose 291 gallery on 5th Avenue helped make photography an accepted art form (and who was also married to Georgia O'Keeffe). The holdings grew with a master set of prints of Edward Steichen's work and the complete personal collection of Walker Evans.

The same ticket gets you into the Cloisters, a hundred blocks north in Fort Tyron Park overlooking the Hudson River. This medieval fantasia was built by John D. Rockefeller from the Cuxa, Bonnefont, Trie, and Saint-Guilhem cloisters, excavated in France and reconstructed here. It's a less-traveled spot that's also a quiet favorite of many New Yorkers, and it houses the *Unicorn Tapestries*—a mysterious narrative that may be the finest surviving example of medieval embroidery in the world.

In 2017, the Met opened the Met Breuer in the building that the Whitney Museum had lived in since 1966. The Brutalist masterpiece by architect Marcel Breuer is one of the earliest examples of a museum's building being a work of art in and of itself (it followed Frank Lloyd Wright's Guggenheim Museum [p. 46] by 7 years).

18

Neue Galerie

1048 5TH AVENUE
NEW YORK, NY 10028

Perhaps the most specific museum in Manhattan, the Neue Galerie devotes one floor of a Beaux-Arts mansion to early 20th-century work from Vienna, and another floor to work from the same period in Germany. Gustav Klimt and Egon Schiele are the big stars of the show here, and it is a jewelbox of a museum.

Though Klimt's *The Kiss* isn't here, another famous "Golden era" painting of his is—the portrait of Adele Bloch-Bauer, the subject of a story that became the cause célèbre for Nazi-confiscated art. The rest of the floor continues with the Vienna Secessionists, and includes Schiele's self-portraits, as well as work by Alfred Kubin and Oskar Kokoschka. It also displays Wiener Werkstätte works—the cross-disciplinary art and design group, founded by Koloman Moser and Josef Hoffmann, which included work by Adolf Loos and Otto Wagner.

The German floor rotates permanent-collection items from the movements, including Die Brücke (Emile Nolde and Ernst Ludwig Kirchner), Der Blaue Reiter (Franz Marc und Gabriele Münter), and the Neue Sachlichkeit movement (Max Beckmann, Otto Dix, Christian Schad, and George Grosz).

The museum is so elegant and grand it seems of a piece with the older Museum Mile spots along Fifth Avenue—but it was only opened in 2001. Its temporary shows continue to dig and shine light on this heady era.

INSTALLATION VIEW OF GUSTAV KLIMT, *PORTRAIT OF ADELE BLOCH-BAUER I*, FLANKED BY GEORGE MINNE SCULPTURES.
PHOTO: HULYA KOLABAS FOR NEUE GALERIE, NEW YORK

The Frick Collection

1 EAST 70TH STREET
NEW YORK, NY 10021

A perfect museum in every way, the Gilded Age mansion once owned by Pittsburgh industrialist Henry Clay Frick holds a small collection of world-renowned Old Master paintings in opulent salons and drawing rooms often hung the way Frick himself left them on his death in 1919. The collection includes the risqué, multi-panel *The Progress of Love* by Jean-Honoré Fragonard in its own Rococo room, and another full room of François Boucher panels. On a more serious note, there are major portraits by Titian, Hans Holbein the Younger, El Greco, Diego Velázquez, Rembrandt, and Jean-Auguste-Dominique Ingres's intimate masterpiece *Louise de Broglie, Countess d'Haussonville.* There are 3 Vermeer paintings, including *Mistress and Maid.* Moving along, there are paintings by Francisco Goya, Édouard Manet, James Abbott McNeill Whistler, Jean-Baptiste-Camille Corot, Jean-Baptiste-Siméon Chardin, Pierre-Auguste Renoir, Paolo Veronese, and J. M. W. Turner to see, as well. Sadly, younger art lovers in your party will have to wait outside—you must be at least 10 years old to enter.

NEARBY: Assuming a visit to the museums just a few blocks north have already been taken care of, stroll downtown toward the Park Avenue Armory (646 Park Avenue). It's not the one where the famous Armory Show of 1913 expanded Americans' view of modern art—that's at 26th Street and Lexington Avenue. But it does present site-specific contemporary art and performance pieces. Recent ones have included collaborations between architects Herzog & de Meuron and Ai Weiwei, a massive drawing made with a fleet of motorcycles by Aaron Rose, and a multimedia exhibition by musician and performance artist Laurie Anderson. Also just steps away is the Carlyle Hotel, where you can enjoy a cocktail under murals drawn by illustrator and bon vivant Ludwig Bemelmans; he made them in exchange for a half-year's worth of accommodations for his family.

INSTALLATION VIEW OF JEAN-AUGUSTE-DOMINIQUE INGRES, *COMTESSE D'HAUSSONVILLE*, 1845, OIL ON CANVAS, 51⅞ × 36¼ IN. THE FRICK COLLECTION, NEW YORK, NY.
PHOTO: MICHAEL BODYCOMB

The Museum of Modern Art

11 WEST 53RD STREET
NEW YORK, NY 10019

MOMA PS1
22-25 JACKSON AVENUE
LONG ISLAND CITY, NY 11101

It's notable that the name of the Museum of Modern Art doesn't contain any geographic location. It doesn't need to: MoMA, as it's known, is considered the single most important museum for modern art in the world. If it only had Pablo Picasso's *Les Demoiselles D'Avingon*, you'd need to visit. If it only had Vincent van Gogh's *Starry Night*, you'd have to visit. Henri Matisse's *L'Atelier Rouge* would also compel a visit on its own.

MoMA's got a ton of history, and Monets to burn (it actually accidentally torched an 18-foot-long *Water Lilies* in 1958, and replaced it with another a couple years later). The Modern, founded by Abby Aldrich Rockefeller and a group of ladies in 1929, is the kind of museum that didn't just gather its treasures, but made the case for modern art as it was happening. Originally on the 12th floor of a 5th Avenue office building, it landed at its current 53rd Street location, designed in the International Style by Edward Durell Stone and Philip L. Goodwin, in 1939. Its iconic garden, with a Picasso goat, an Art Nouveau Paris metro entrance, and Aristide Maillol's famous tumbling nymph, was soon added by Philip Johnson.

In the 1930s, the museum's first director, Alfred H. Barr Jr., staged the first American retrospective of van Gogh and one of the first on Picasso—blockbuster shows that influenced how we think about their genius and shaped the world's view of modern art as a whole. MoMA's first director of photography was Edward Steichen, who put together one of the most famous photo shows of all time, *The Family of Man*, which toured the world for 8 years. The museum has also pioneered the treatment of architecture and design as worthy of museum attention, with a collection spanning Frank Lloyd Wright's furniture to Ettore Sottsass and Perry King's Olivetti typewriter (and, since it's always growing, the inevitable onslaught of Apple products). MoMA's film department is also incredibly important.

The expansion in the early 2000s, planned by Diller Scofidio + Renfro and architect Yoshio Taniguchi, finally gave MoMA the grandeur its influence merits: soaring atriums, space for Barnett Newman's *Broken Obelisk* to loom menacingly over the crowds waiting to get in, and massive reinforced gallery spaces where multi-ton pieces, like Richard Serra's *Torqued Ellipses*, can be loaded in by crane without fear of causing a collapse.

It's not unusual to hear a visitor talk about the high monetary value of key paintings—and for the selfie-obsessed to spoil the experience. *Les Demoiselles d'Avignon* and *Starry Night* are the ones you'll fight to get near. But the museum's collection has so many pleasures, repeat visits never

disappoint: There are Frida Kahlo's *Self-Portrait with Cropped Hair* and Piet Mondrian's *Broadway Boogie Woogie*, and the always wonderful sensation of seeing Oskar Schlemmer's *Bauhaus Stairway* hanging above a staircase of the original building.

Across the East River, MoMA also runs PS1—a contemporary art space in industrial Long Island City set in a Romanesque Revival school building from 1893. Primarily known for its boundary-pushing temporary exhibitions and its courtyard—where annual Young Architects Program installations become the settings for the popular summer Warm Up dance parties—PS1 has several permanent, site-specific pieces intermingled with its authentic, midcentury New York City school décor, including signage by Lawrence Weiner and Robert Artschwager; stairwells with murals by William Kentridge, Cecily Brown, and Ernesto Cavalo; and pieces involving holes in the wall or floors by Pipilotti Rist, Alexis Rockman, and, the oldest intervention in the space, Alan Saret from 1976. James Turrell's *Meeting* is open to the sky on the top floor—his second-ever Skyspace, which opened in 1986, has undergone recent renovations. After-hours visits are available Monday nights by reservation in months when the weather is good.

SCULPTURE GARDEN, THE MUSEUM OF MODERN ART, NEW YORK, NY.
PHOTO: © ANTON HAVELAAR/123RF.COM

WISDOM AND KNOWLEDGE SHALL BE THE STABILITY OF THY TIMES

21

Rockefeller Center

45 ROCKEFELLER PLAZA
NEW YORK, NY 10111

An Art Deco fantasia at the heart of Midtown Manhattan, Rockefeller Center holds dozens of treasures and is considered one of America's finest creative moments during the Great Depression. When it was being built, some hated it (the *New Yorker* critic Lewis Mumford claimed it caused him to flee the city for several years) and some were surprisingly kind (famed architect Le Corbusier praised it for being rational and harmonious). Put together by a consortium of several architectural firms, it's arguably the consistent vision of the art elements that bind it all together. And since the developer John D. Rockefeller and his family were already deep in the arts—with Abby Aldrich Rockefeller having founded the Museum of Modern Art (p. 56), and the whole gang having stuffed their Hudson River mansion, Kykuit, with masterpieces—they got it mostly right.

A mythology professor named Hartley Burr Alexander had built a business for himself as an "iconographer"—art directing relief sculptures and writing inscriptions for buildings of the era nationwide— and it was his grand, romantic vision that carried through the project, though he was so maniacal he had to be canned early on. Lee Lawrie designed 12 major pieces, including the 45-foot-high freestanding *Atlas*, in collaboration with Zig-Zag Moderne style specialist Rene Paul Chambellan. Directly behind it, over the door to the RCA building (now known as 30 Rock), is one of Lawrie's best works in the complex, *Wisdom*.

Dozens of artists participated: Paul Manship's *Prometheus*, in gilded bronze, became one of the most famous symbols of New York City, and dominates the main plaza (and its skating rink). Isamu Noguchi's *News*, a stainless-steel ode to the labor of journalism, above the entrance to the Associated Press building, is perhaps the most modern piece in the complex (and a very rare figurative piece for him). Among the many others involved are Gaston Lachaise, Leo Friedlander, and Margaret Bourke-White, who filled a rotunda of 30 Rock with a wraparound photo mural.

Murals dominate Radio City—where Abby got interior designer Donald Deskey hired—and are worth paying for a tour to see. They include a 2,400-square-foot mural in the foyer by Ezra Winter, a men's room by Stuart Davis (technically owned by MoMA), and a ladies' room by Yasuo Kuniyoshi, who had to be called in to replace Georgia O'Keeffe. Architect Edward Durell Stone is responsible for the theater's most striking visual effect—the clean, circular proscenium that echoes outward, blending seamlessly with the ceiling.

The most famous art-history moment at Rockefeller Center is lost forever. Coming off the success (and seeming blurring of his Socialist hard edges) of his *Detroit Industry* murals (p. 129), Diego Rivera was brought in by Abby to fill the lobby of 30 Rock with a 67-foot painting. It was the most prominent place for art in the entire complex, and Rivera had edged out Matisse and Picasso, whom Abby's son Nelson had put forth. The mural was a complicated mix of contrasting social visions, involving labor, race, wealth, industry, science, and pretty much everything else. Rivera included a May Day march with a portrait of Lenin in it—and that's when the shit hit the fan. After major battles in the media and behind closed doors, during which Rivera refused to remove Lenin, the entire mural was destroyed. Today, a replacement by José Maria Sert still stands.

The tradition for very large art continues. In Rockefeller Center's East of 6th Avenue section, the Equitable Center's AXA collection features a 66-foot-tall painting by Roy Lichtenstein, *Mural with Blue Brushstroke*; a 4-story Sol LeWitt wall drawing; and work by James Rosenquist, Barry Flanagan, and Agnes Denes. Another loss: In what was once the high-powered Palio restaurant, wraparound paintings by Sandro Chia illustrated the famous horserace at Siena; though they are said to be extant, the space has been renovated without them. But there will always be more. Rockefeller Center sponsors annual installations of very, very large artworks, which have included Jeff Koons, Chris Burden, Elmgreen & Dragset, and Tim Noble and Sue Webster, in conjunction with public-art powerhouse Art Production Fund.

NEARBY: At the stately St. Regis Hotel on 55th Street across 5th Avenue, there's a magnificent treasure hidden in the bar. A luminous mural by Maxfield Parrish, the painter and illustrator best known for his languid nymphs basking in twilight, hangs above the bar. Commissioned for the Knickerbocker Hotel in 1904, the assignment called for the face of its owner, Josef Astor, to stand in for Old King Cole of nursery-rhyme fame. As seen on the faces of his "fiddlers three," the king has made a flatulent gaffe.

22

Whitney Museum of American Art

99 GANSEVOORT ST
NEW YORK, NY 10014

One of the things the art world loves to hate—and that turns everyone in New York into snarky critics—is the Whitney Biennial. The show of contemporary art pulled together by guest curators never fails to attract flack, but it also never fails to launch a few careers, or remind people of some forgotten ones. It seems unlikely that that ability to stay right in the cultural hot zone where art can make trouble was born of a socialite's collecting Ashcan School paintings a hundred years ago—but getting right up in the fray was Gertrude Vanderbilt Whitney's mission from the start. That that energy has also recently delivered one of the best spaces for both old and new art in the world—in its newest quarters by Renzo Piano—is also astounding.

Created in reaction to the Museum of Modern Art's obsessive love of the Europeans, the Whitney Museum had its roots in the Whitney Studio Club that Gertrude Whitney started in 1918 in Greenwich Village. She jumped right into controversy when she became a patron of John Sloan and his Ashcan gang—when their gritty realism was seen as anathema. She stuck with American painters as modernism flourished, with additions by Charles Demuth, Edward Hopper,

Stuart Davis, and Charles Sheeler. In 1929, annoyed by the MoMA's Europhilia, Whitney used her 700-piece collection to start her own formal museum—and kept up with every major movement in American art through American Scene painters like Thomas Hart Benton, Raphael Soyer, Grant Wood, and Charles Burchfield, to Abstract Expressionists, Pop Artists, color-field painters, and the Post-Minimalists.

The collection wound up in an iconic building on Madison Avenue in 1966—the Brutalist masterpiece by Marcel Breuer (that is now the Met Breuer, p. 49). A few generations of New York children know it best for its permanent installation of Alexander Calder's *Circus* on a hard-to-find mezzanine floor, but it has also kept major works by Mark Rothko, Eva Hesse, Louise Bourgeois, Helen Frankenthaler, Frank Stella, Franz Kline, and Robert Motherwell in heavy rotation. Its deepest holdings are in the works of Georgie O'Keeffe, Jasper Johns, Agnes Martin, Claes Oldenburg, Ed Ruscha, Lorna Simpson, Cindy Sherman, David Wojnarowicz, and a lot more Calder. Its photography collection wasn't started until 1991, but includes the work of Margaret Bourke-White, William Eggleston, and Imogen Cunningham.

The Whitney has since moved to a new, instant architectural landmark by Renzo Piano in the Meatpacking District, not far from its Bohemian roots in the Village. Though the exterior doesn't look like anything without the sunset reflecting on it, the interiors have been praised for having perfect

light and space for the Whitney's collection—art that is sometimes too ungainly and strange for an average gallery space, and art that has been tucked away for too long in dark spaces and deserves more room. One of the biggest accolades the Whitney has received in relation to the move is that by creating such vast space, it hasn't just enabled crazier, more populist stunts, but instead has allowed the museum to bring lesser-known masterpieces forward to hang side by side with the Pollocks, Hoppers, and O'Keeffes. The Whitney also deserves a place on the mental art map of America for its Independent Study Program, which helped launch the careers of artists such as Julian Schnabel, Jenny Holzer, Rirkrit Tiravanija, Felix Gonzalez-Torres, Katharina Sieverding, Ashley Bickerton, and Sarah Morris, as well as beloved *New York Times* art critic Roberta Smith.

NEARBY: Head north from the Whitney along the High Line, a public park upcycled from an old railroad overpass by architects Diller Scofidio + Renfro with landscape architects James Corner Field Operations and Piet Oudolf, and you'll find the epicenter of Manhattan's gallery scene (from approximately 19th Street to 27th Street between 10th and 11th Avenues). You can happily wander in and out—some are the size of small museums.

EXTERIOR VIEW OF THE WHITNEY MUSEUM OF AMERICAN ART FROM GANSEVOORT STREET, NEW YORK, NY.

PHOTO: ED LEDERMAN, 2015

negro sun shine

Downtown New York City

BELOW 23RD STREET
NEW YORK, NY

It used to be that art went uptown to cash in and piss in the fireplaces of the rich (as Jackson Pollock did). Downtown was the Village, SoHo, the Lower East Side, and neighborhoods that real-estate agents hadn't bothered to name yet. That order to the universe fell apart a long time ago, as the money came downtown and made things too expensive for artists. Old story, but New York, as remorseless as it can be about change, can't quite erase it all. Keep heading downtown and you'll get to money again—and a few commissioned corporate and public-art projects worth the trip. Here's a shaggy tour of some of the art sites that matter.

A. THE FACTORY (33 UNION SQUARE WEST). Andy Warhol's studio took over the sixth floor of the Decker Building on Union Square West in 1967. Two of his most famous films were shot entirely here, *Flesh* and *Trash*, and his circle, which included Viva, Ultra Violet, Holly Woodlawn, Candy Darling, and Billy Name, attracted artists like Ray Johnson, Stephen Shore, Rene Ricard, John Giorno, and, later, Jean-Michel Basquiat and Keith Haring. This is where Valerie Solanas shot Warhol in 1968.

B. MAX'S KANSAS CITY (213 PARK AVENUE SOUTH). Made famous in part by the Velvet Underground, who recorded their last ever performance there. Max's had already established its art bona fides soon after opening in 1963, counting John Chamberlain, Robert Rauschenberg, and Larry Rivers as regulars. Dozens followed: Carl Andre, Dan Graham, Robert Smithson, Joseph Kosuth, Roy Lichtenstein, Donald Judd, Dan Flavin, Richard Serra, and heavy-hitting critics Robert Hughes, Clement Greenberg, and Harold Rosenberg. When Warhol moved the Factory a block away, his crew made itself at home, too. In the '70s Robert Mapplethorpe would come see his girlfriend, Patti Smith, play—until it closed in 1973.

C. CEDAR TAVERN (24 UNIVERSITY PLACE). Replaced by an NYU dorm and a CVS drugstore, this is the location of the pub that attracted the earlier generation of the New York School—Jackson Pollock, Willem de Kooning, Mark Rothko, and Franz Kline—for nightly brawls.

D. MCSORLEY'S (15 EAST 7TH STREET). One more bar and an ever-early group of boozing artists. In this pub, open since 1854, Ashcanners George Luks and John Sloan were regulars, along with Stuart Davis. Sloan's painting of the bar hangs at the Detroit Institute of Arts (p. 129). The sawdust is still on the floor and the facial hair in the painting is back in style—the only difference is the bar began allowing women in 1970.

E. EDWARD HOPPER STUDIO (3 WASHINGTON SQUARE NORTH). The moody painter lived and worked with his wife, Jo, on the fourth floor of this townhouse from 1913 to 1967. His original easel and printing press are here, along with portraits of the couple by Arnold Newman and Berenice Abbott. Visit by appointment through NYU's Silver School of Social Work by calling Amanda Lorencz at 212-998-5900.

F. JUDSON MEMORIAL CHURCH (WASHINGTON SQUARE SOUTH). The Stanford White–designed church, with windows by John La Farge and sculptures by Augustus Saint-Gaudens, became a hotbed of civil rights activism in the 1950s, and made it a mission to support experimental artists and their radical messages. It provided studio spaces for Claes Oldenburg, Robert Rauschenberg, Jim Dine, and the happenings that the open, interdisciplinary mix of creative people around supported.

G. PABLO PICASSO'S *BUST OF SYLVETTE* (505 LAGUARDIA PLACE). To complement his pair of Brutalist dorm towers for NYU, I. M. Pei had a bust Picasso made in 1934 re-created in concrete 6 stories tall. Good Cubist fun but the sign says, "Do not touch."

H. FORREST MYERS'S *THE WALL* (599 BROADWAY). A Minimalist artwork, 8 stories tall, that consists of steel beams bolted to a blue wall. Throughout the 2000s, the piece was the focus of a battle that pitted the first amendment against the fifth, and involved the work being taken down and eventually restored.

I. KEITH HARING'S POP SHOP (292 LAFAYETTE STREET). The first store Haring opened, in 1986, to sell small editions based on his work that he intended to get in the hands of "the people" in the same way his subway drawings were public. It closed in 2005, and now operates online to support the Keith Haring Foundation. The ceiling has been preserved in the lobby of the New York Historical Society.

J. FOOD (127 PRINCE STREET). The site of an artist-run restaurant from the days when art ruled these streets. The neighborhood has the greatest collection of 19th-century cast iron buildings in the world—buildings whose innovations in steel allowed taller ceilings, more light, and more floor space for everything from department stores to textile factories. By the mid-20th century, the area had become rundown and known as Hell's Hundred Acres, and so artists came for the cheap space. Over time, a community developed. Gordon Matta-Clark, Carol Goodden, and Tina Girouard opened this gathering place in 1971. Clarke cut holes in the walls and artists such as Donald Judd and composer John Cage were invited to be guest chefs. By 1973, the neighborhood had been named SoHo, and for a couple of decades became the home of the city's top galleries before high-fashion stores chased them to Chelsea in the late '90s.

K. WALTER DE MARIA'S *EARTH ROOM* (141 WOOSTER STREET). Built in 1977, the Land Art artist filled a 3,600-square-foot loft with dirt, 22 inches deep. Visitors stood at a glass partition and breathed in the heady scent in the middle of the city. (In 1980, the Dia Foundation adopted the piece.)

L. CHASE MANHATTAN PLAZA (PINE STREET). In the late 1960s, David Rockefeller commissioned 2 pieces for his bank's new building. The first was Isamu Noguchi's *Sunken Garden*, inspired by Zen meditation gardens like the Ryoanji Temple in Kyoto; the second was Jean Dubuffet's *Group of Four Trees*. Noguchi's striking *Red Cube* is a block away, at 140 Broadway.

M. LOUISE NEVELSON PLAZA (AT MAIDEN LANE). The sculptor built the imposing *Shadows and Flags*—70 feet of Cor-Ten steel—for this site in 1977, at age 70, along with six 20-foot-tall pieces. In 2010, it was renovated with some dubious, sleek glass benches.

N. TOM OTTERNESS'S *THE REAL WORLD* (BATTERY PARK). Ostensibly a children's park, the sculptor has snuck allegorical lessons on greed, racism, sexism, and capitalism among his cute bronze characters.

O. JULIE MEHRETU'S *MURAL* AT GOLDMAN SACHS (200 WEST STREET). The painter's 80-foot-long by 23-foot-tall mural was called "the most ambitious painting I've seen in a dozen years" by the *New Yorker*'s Calvin Tompkins. It's pure energy—better than a jolt of espresso on the way to work.

P. DOUG AND MIKE STARN SUBWAY STATION INTERIOR (SOUTH FERRY TERMINAL). The twin photographers were given the run of the station by the MTA and created an all-over experience with layered glass photos of trees and roots and veiny leaves, mixed with maps of Manhattan, old and new.

Q. RACHEL WHITEREAD'S *CABIN* (GOVERNORS ISLAND). In the Hills section of Governors Island, within sight of both the Statue of Liberty and the bottom of Manhattan, the British artist has installed a permanent site-specific piece made of cast concrete. It's kind of Unabomber-style, kind of rustic New England cute. Intrigue with a view.

23

The Noguchi Museum

9-01 33RD ROAD
LONG ISLAND CITY, NY 11106

One of the best single-artist museums in the United States, the Noguchi Museum benefits from the artist, Isamu Noguchi, having designed it side by side with the building's architect in the 1980s. It grew out of an old photogravure factory across the street from his studio, and is organized around a 75-year-old "Tree of Life" tree. The spaces weave inside and out, allowing for large outdoor sculptures and fountains to have equal footing with the gallery displays of sculptures, paper lanterns, and furniture. The inventive layout also guides the visitor through Noguchi's many mediums, giving the museum the feeling of being much bigger than it is.

Noguchi was born in Los Angeles to an American mother and Japanese father and then moved to Japan for his first 13 years. It was a show of Constantin Brancusi sculptures that changed his life in 1926, and led him to move to Paris on a Guggenheim Fellowship to work in the master's studio. It's easy to see Noguchi as the successor to much of what Brancusi sought to do: In the older artist's famous *Bird in Space*, he makes marble seem to soar, distilling avian movement perfectly and without need of representation. Noguchi coaxed movement from all kinds of marble, granite, and many other types of material.

Based in New York for most of his life, Noguchi traveled constantly, collaborated with choreographers such as Martha Graham and Merce Cunningham and the composer John Cage. He also designed objects for companies like Zenith Radio and Herman Miller Furniture—his coffee table is an icon of midcentury-modern design.

While he's not thought of as a Japanese artist, Noguchi worked in Japan at times, and even voluntarily joined the Japanese internment camps in the West during World War II, in

protest of the camps and in support of the patriotism of Japanese Americans. His explorations of traditional Japanese paper-lantern construction are perhaps his best known works, and are available at the museum store.

The museum creates and hosts very smart temporary shows—an exhibition reveals Alexander Calder's obsession with chess, for instance, or the Japanese modernist Kenmochi Isamu's wicker chairs. It also uses its serene garden to put on excellent public programs, including lively sculpture workshops for children.

NEARBY: Visitors can explore Socrates Sculpture Park, a ramshackle, riverside alternative art space anchored by a giant Mark di Suvero sculpture and seasonal shows of site-specific pieces that verge on being punk rock personified. The Museum of the Moving Image and MoMA's PS1 branch (p. 56) are also nearby.

INSTALLATION VIEWS OF SELECTED SCULPTURES BY ISAMU NOGUCHI FROM 1969–83, NOGUCHI MUSEUM, LONG ISLAND CITY, NY.

PHOTOS: NICK KNIGHT, © THE ISAMU NOGUCHI FOUNDATION AND GARDEN MUSEUM, NEW YORK / ARS

24

Brooklyn Museum

200 EASTERN PARKWAY
BROOKLYN, NY 11238

At a half-million square feet, the Brooklyn Museum is another New York City encyclopedic museum experience that can easily absorb more than one visit. Though the institution has struggled over the years financially and received criticism for its embrace of pop-culture blockbusters like shows devoted to *Star Wars* or sneaker culture, its collections and temporary exhibitions are outstanding, and make it an essential visit.

The museum opened in its Beaux-Arts McKim, Mead & White building in 1895 after consolidating various Brooklyn-based cultural institutions dating back another 70 years. Its pediment sculptures were designed by Daniel Chester French of Lincoln Memorial fame (and he made the allegorical sculptures that flank the entrance on both ends of the Manhattan Bridge). But inside the museum's updated entrance pavilion, things very quickly feel more up-to-date as you encounter several large paintings by Kehinde Wiley, known for putting young African American men in the genre of historic military equestrian portraits. (Notably, the Brooklyn Museum was the first institution to collect the artist's work. In spring 2018, Wiley was in the news for his wildly inventive official portrait of former president Barack Obama.)

On a mezzanine, another eye-popping bit of neo-realist painting awaits—the museum's 2004 commission of a mural by Alexis Rockman that shows a post-apocalyptic Brooklyn, flooded because of global warming.

The vast history covered in the museum is impressive: Its earliest ancient Egyptian object is the mysterious, predynastic, terracotta bird woman, and it was early to collect African and Pacific Islander art, having started in 1900. There's a gallery of Rodin sculptures looking perfectly at ease in a Neoclassical rotunda, and there's a maze of historic rooms recreating American interiors of many eras. The collection of American art has been used in ingenious ways, and includes one of the famous paintings *Peaceable Kingdom* by Edward Hicks and *Eight Bells* by Winslow Homer, as well as key works by Georgia O'Keeffe and Mary Cassatt.

The real one-of-a-kind moment here is Judy Chicago's *The Dinner Party*—a room-size installation and masterpiece of feminist art created originally from 1974 to 1979. In a dark room, a triangular table hosts elaborate settings designated for feminist heroes, real and fictional, throughout history, from Eleanor of Aquitaine, Susan B. Anthony, and Sojourner Truth, to painters Artemisia Gentileschi and Georgia O'Keeffe, to writers Virginia Woolf and Emily Dickinson, and on and on. Each place setting has a symbolic porcelain piece—often suggestive of female anatomy—customized utensils, and an embroidered cloth.

HERE
LIE
THE
SECRETS
OF THE
VISITORS
OF
GREEN-WOOD
CEMETERY

NEARBY: Back at the corner of Flatbush Avenue and Eastern Parkway in Grand Army Plaza, you'll find one of the finest examples of academic history sculpture in Augustus Saint-Gaudens's last major work, an equestrian sculpture memorializing William Tecumseh Sherman. But there's a classical sculpture with a twist across town at Green-wood Cemetery (500 25th Street, Brooklyn), where a monument by contemporary artist Sophie Calle looks perfectly of a piece with the other stone obelisks and slabs dating back to the 1800s. The inscription on the white marble spire says, "Here Lie the Secrets of the Visitors of Green-Wood Cemetery." People are invited to write their confessions and slip them in a mailbox slot at the base, which the artist—whom one critic called, "the Marcel Duchamp of emotional dirty laundry"—will occasionally collect and burn. The piece was a commission from Creative Time, a nonprofit responsible for some of the most exciting public art projects in New York City. Calle is in good company at Green-wood: A tour of other monuments reveals the work of Daniel Chester French, Saint-Gaudens, and John Quincy Adams Ward. You can also visit the grave of 1980s Neo-Expressionist art star Jean-Michel Basquiat.

PAGES 68–69: JUDY CHICAGO, *THE DINNER PARTY*, 1979, WITH "WING 2," FEATURING ELIZABETH R, ARTEMISIA GENTILESCHI, AND ANNA VAN SCHURMAN PLACE SETTINGS. COLLECTION OF THE BROOKLYN MUSEUM; GIFT OF THE ELIZABETH A. SACKLER FOUNDATION. © JUDY CHICAGO/ ARTIST RIGHTS SOCIETY (ARS) NY.

PHOTO: © DONALD WOODMAN/ARS NY

LEFT: SOPHIE CALLE, *HERE LIE THE SECRETS OF GREEN-WOOD CEMETERY*, A PROJECT BY CREATIVE TIME. GREEN-WOOD CEMETERY, BROOKLYN, NY.

PHOTO: GUILLAUME ZICCARELLI, COURTESY THE ARTIST AND PERROTIN

25

Pollock-Krasner House and Study Center

830 SPRINGS FIREPLACE ROAD
EAST HAMPTON, NY 11937

The home and studio where Jackson Pollock and Lee Krasner lived and worked is quite simply the most vital historical artist studio that can be visited today. The modest, shingled country cottage where the couple moved in 1946 with a loan from Peggy Guggenheim—in part to help Pollock stop his debauchery and focus on work—is preserved exactly as Krasner left it after her death in 1984 (much of it the same as before Pollock's death in 1956). It's got their furniture, his stereo and jazz records, her dress and books.

There's some original work of theirs here, too—a self-portrait by Krasner, and Pollock's *Composition with Red Arc and Horses* from 1938, which manages to show both his interest in Native American artwork discovered while working for the WPA in the Southwest and his short time learning from David Alfaro Siqueiros when he held classes in New York City.

But the studio—an uninsulated shack—is what really gets the adrenalin going. On the floor are Pollock's splatters—he developed his all-over splatter style here, and painted his most famous paintings, like *Autumn Rhythm*. The smears and drips on the wall are Krasner's. Though she was already a mature artist when she and Pollock got together, her career and development were slowed by her efforts to support him. So she made her most important paintings—big, sensuous, warm abstractions with collage elements, like *Milkweed* (now at the Albright-Knox Art Gallery, p. 38) and *Imperative* (now at the National Gallery of Art, p. 96)—after his death, when she started working in the studio instead of a small second bedroom. Paint cans and knives and brushes used by both artists are here and look ready to be picked up and put to use again any moment.

The house is operated by Stony Brook University and the Pollock-Krasner Foundation and it puts on temporary shows of its own collections and other relevant work. It's only open from May to October.

INTERIOR VIEW OF JACKSON POLLOCK'S STUDIO, POLLOCK-KRASNER HOUSE AND STUDY CENTER, EAST HAMPTON, NY.

PHOTO: HELEN A. HARRISON

Parrish Art Museum

279 MONTAUK HIGHWAY
WATER MILL, NY 11976

A barn 2 football fields long houses the Parrish Art Museum, designed to hold almost 120 years of art made in the Hamptons. The architects, Jacques Herzog and Pierre de Meuron, tweaked the roof and windows to let the same light that drew artists to the East End in the first place illuminate the museum's art.

The museum was founded, 2 locations ago, in part because of American Impressionist William Merritt Chase, who was running an art school nearby in the 1890s. One of the most influential art teachers in America, he would, at one time or another, teach George Bellows, Charles Demuth, Lydia Field Emmet, Marsden Hartley, Georgia O'Keeffe, and John Marin. His first Manhattan school would eventually become the Parsons School of Art and Design. The Parrish holds the biggest and most important collection of Chase's work, including *Park in Brooklyn* and *Blue Kimono*.

The mission here has held steady: Only artists with studios from the area need apply. Fortunately, the area attracts well-heeled art stars who have already made it big in the city. The collection grew to include Larry Rivers, Alfonso A. Ossorio, Helen Frankenthaler, Alice Aycock, Lynda Benglis, Dorothea Rockburne,

Mary Heilmann, Jennifer Bartlett, Malcolm Morley, April Gornik, Eric Fischl, and Cindy Sherman. It also has a large Roy Lichtenstein sculpture on its 14-acre site: *Tokyo Brushstroke I & II*.

In 1975, the museum received a major bequest of 250 works of realist painter Fairfield Porter, including *Laurence at the Piano* and *Jane and Elizabeth*. Far from a reactionary, Porter appreciated (and was friends with) the Abstract Expressionists, especially Willem de Kooning.

NEARBY: The LongHouse Reserve (133 Hands Creek Road, East Hampton) is 16 acres of sculpture gardens built around a house inspired by 7th-century Shinto shrines in Japan. Its most notable piece is Buckminster Fuller's Fly's Eye Dome. (Though Fuller is known as an architect, this is undeniably a sculpture.) Work by Yoko Ono, de Kooning, and many more rounds out the gardens.

INSTALLATION VIEW OF WORKS FROM THE PERMANENT COLLECTION, PARRISH ART MUSEUM, WATER MILL, NY.

PHOTO: IWAN BAAN

The Dan Flavin Art Institute

23 CORWITH AVENUE
BRIDGEHAMPTON, NY 11932

A 1908 Craftsman-style firehouse serves as something of a personal scrapbook for the late artist Dan Flavin. In 1983, when the building was remodeled as a gallery, the artist selected pieces of his work dating back to 1961, when he first started working with light fixtures after having been employed as a guard at New York's American Museum of Natural History—it was there that he noticed he was including the light fixtures in his sketches. His first sculptures involving lighting were created that year and within 2 years he would create *Diagonal of Personal Ecstasy (the Diagonal of May 25, 1963)*, dedicated to Constantin Brancusi, using the commercially available fluorescent tubes that would be his medium for the rest of his life.

Every piece at the windowless venue is in a custom-built space, making for a seamless experience. Unlike the massive spaces full of large Flavin installations at Dia:Beacon and in Marfa, Texas, the intimacy and quick-paced retrospective gives visitors a sense of the surprising variety in his work. There are installations that create immersive color baths, some with intense light, some that are crisp, and some more blurred in their effects. Some are blunt and seem to be all about their structure, and some are mysterious. Some may even hint at silliness. Flavin was an unusual kind of insider in New York's art scene. He studied at the Hans Hofmann School, he worked in the mailroom at the Guggenheim Museum, and ran the elevator at MoMA where he met Sol LeWitt and Robert Ryman. Many of his works were in homage to other artists such as Piet Mondrian or Russian Constructivist sculptor Vladimir Tatlin. So it's fitting he should have his own museum near the city.

The Institute is run by the Dia Foundation and stages temporary shows in a gallery space, as well; recent exhibitions have included work by Mary Heilmann and Keith Sonnier. The firehouse was a church for many years, and it's a bit of serendipitous fun that its neon cross was saved and is on display in a back room.

EXTERIOR VIEW OF THE DAN FLAVIN ART INSTITUTE, BRIDGEHAMPTON, NY.

PHOTO: BILL JACOBSON STUDIO, NY, COURTESY DIA ART FOUNDATION, NY

The Andy Warhol Museum

117 SANDUSKY STREET
PITTSBURGH, PA 15212

THE CARNEGIE MUSEUM OF ART
FORBES AVENUE
PITTSBURGH, PA 15213

Seven floors of an industrial warehouse make this the largest single artist–devoted museum in America (next on the list is Florida's Dalí Museum, p. 116), and with its basement activity center, the Factory, makes it one of the most fun and vital. Plans for the museum in the city of the Pop artist's birth began about 2 years after his death in 1986, and got off the ground with a donation of works from the Dia Foundation worth some $80 million at the time.

Everything is here. Marilyn, Elvis, Liz, the Disasters, silkscreens, paintings, Brillo boxes, silver balloons, the early blotted-line drawings, prints of all 315 films (over 4,000 more moving images, if you count videos), and the "time capsules" Warhol assembled of day-to-day items.

If you've become cynical about Warhol due to high auction prices or too many comparisons of him to Kim Kardashian, the underground section might refresh your view: It doesn't feature the sex, drugs & rock 'n' roll of Warhol's original Manhattan studios (see p. 63), but it does facilitate creativity in many forms: Constant workshops run by deeply knowledgeable artists and educators let visitors of all ages and abilities make silkscreens and drawings with the techniques the artist used.

The Warhol Museum is partners with the Carnegie Museum of Art, an institution that is at once more traditional and even more forward-looking. Established in 1895 by industrialist Andrew Carnegie, whose directive was to "collect the Old Masters of tomorrow," the museum holds collections across all fields and continents, including highlights such as Winslow Homer's *The Wreck* and Vincent van Gogh's *Wheat Fields After the Rain (The Plain of Auvers)*. But it also puts on the Carnegie International triennial, a show whose early juries included Alfred H. Barr Jr., Pierre Bonnard, Thomas Eakins, Robert Henri, and Winslow Homer, and which became a barometer of contemporary art when it gave Henri Matisse its first prize in 1927. The show has been the gateway into the museum's collection for many artists, including Cindy Sherman, Mike Kelley, Louise Bourgeois, Richard Serra, and local hero Warhol himself.

The museum's collections are vast, and feature major paintings and sculptures, but it's also strong in very specific niches, such as post-war studio glass (with work by Carlo Scarpa, Sonja Blomdahl, and Toni Zuccheri) and photography (its collection includes the work of W. Eugene Smith, who documented Pittsburgh steel mills extensively for *Life* magazine in the 1940s). One fascinating area of the collection is the complete work—some 80,000 prints—of local African American photographer Charles "Teenie" Harris, who documented the community from 1936 to 1975, including visits from the likes of Muhammad Ali, Louis Armstrong, and John F. Kennedy.

NEARBY: The Mattress Factory (500 Sampsonia Way) started as a live-work space in an old Stearns and Foster building in 1975, and has since grown into a place for experimental art—it calls itself a lab. It has also commissioned 17 permanent installations, including a mirrored and polka-dotted fantasia from Yayoi Kusama, several beautiful light pieces by James Turrell, a dangerous-looking hole in a floor by Sarah Oppenheimer, and a re-creation of transgender artist Greer Lankton's bedroom. It's a beloved spot in the community, and its monthly ARTLabs draw crowds to create work on the fly inspired by current exhibitions.

ANDY WARHOL, *BRILLO SOAP PADS BOX*, 1964. THE ANDY WARHOL MUSEUM, PITTSBURGH, PA

Philadelphia Museum of Art

2600 BENJAMIN FRANKLIN PARKWAY
PHILADELPHIA, PA 19130

Known around the world for 2 macabre works at opposite ends of the spectrum—Thomas Eakins's *The Gross Clinic* and Marcel Duchamp's *Étant Donnés*—it's hard to grasp how much more the Philadelphia Museum of Art holds. It's got the largest collections of both those artists, along with the greatest collection of Brancusi sculptures outside of Europe. It has Paul Cézanne's *The Large Bathers*, Vincent van Gogh's *Sunflowers*, and Pablo Picasso's *Three Musicians*. It has extensive work from the Revolutionary War era, including paintings by all of the talented Peale family—most memorably, Charles Willson Peale's trompe l'oeil of his sons going up life-size stairs, complete with a wooden step breaking the frame. It has collections of Shaker and Pennsylvania-German Arts and Crafts, and a comprehensive look at costume from all over the world. It has massive temple constructions from India and China, and elaborate period rooms of all eras—the highlight being Robert Adams's 1775 drawing room from the Lansdowne House from London with all of its Italian painted panels.

The museum was born out of the Centennial Exposition, marking the signing of the Declaration of Independence in Philadelphia. In 1895, it got its first curatorial department and the donation of a collection of lace. It soon grew out of its space, yet it took over 30 years to finalize plans and open the massive Greek Revival structure it's in today, complete with the grand staircase facing Benjamin Franklin Parkway.

Eakins's painting of Dr. Samuel Gross is considered one of the best American paintings of all time. He painted it with an eye toward showing it in the Centennial, but it was rejected. Duchamp's last art piece, created in secret during a 20-year period when the public thought he had retired from art to play chess, is the eerie *Étant Donnés*; viewed only through a peephole in a wooden door, it's a diorama depicting a woman's body splayed out in some weeds. It was always intended for the Philadelphia Museum of Art—which also had his famous *Fountain* (the shocking Dada readymade signed "R.Mutt") and both *Nude Descending a Staircase* and *The Bride Striped Bare by Her Bachelors, Even*—but it was not installed until after his death in 1969.

Philadelphia must be used to that feeling of delayed gratification: A plan to expand the museum with an addition by Frank Gehry was announced in 2006, but is not scheduled to open until 2028.

NEARBY: The Rodin Museum (2151 Benjamin Franklin Parkway) is operated by the Philadelphia Museum of Art, even though it's down the street and adjacent to the Barnes Foundation's new museum. It's the largest collection of Auguste Rodin's work outside of Paris, and includes the oft-spoofed *The Thinker* out front, the 3-dimensional dorm room poster *The Kiss*, and *The Burghers of Calais*, which the *New Yorker*'s Peter Schjeldahl recently called Rodin's most moving work.

INSTALLATION VIEW OF (**LEFT**) THOMAS EAKINS, *PORTRAIT OF DR. SAMUEL D. GROSS (THE GROSS CLINIC)*, 1875, 8 FT. × 6 FT. 6 IN. GIFT OF THE ALUMNI ASSOCIATION TO JEFFERSON MEDICAL COLLEGE IN 1878 AND PURCHASED BY THE PENNSYLVANIA ACADEMY OF THE FINE ARTS AND THE PHILADELPHIA MUSEUM OF ART IN 2007 WITH THE GENEROUS SUPPORT OF MORE THAN 3,600 DONORS, 2007. PHILADELPHIA MUSEUM OF ART, PHILADELPHIA, PA.

Barnes Foundation

2025 BENJAMIN FRANKLIN PARKWAY
PHILADELPHIA, PA 19130

One of the most controversial museum expansions in the new century was the relocation of Albert Barnes's legendary collection from the suburbs to a gleaming new building by Tod Williams and Billie Tsien in 2012. Lawsuits tried to stop it—the beloved old building was intimate and displayed the art the way Barnes intended. The opening was greeted with much griping; some said the spirit was lost and the building tried too hard to imitate the old one without adding anything worthwhile. But many skeptics were converted. The *New Yorker*'s Peter Schjeldahl wrote, "I couldn't imagine the integrity of the collection...would survive. But it does, magnificently."

The collection was born with the purchase of 2 van Goghs via Barnes's friend William Glackens in 1905, and grew to become one of the most important collections of Impressionism, Post-Impressionism, and early modernism in the world—complemented by African art and decorative objects. On his first trip to Paris, Barnes met Gertrude Stein and bought 2 Matisse paintings, and was soon buying Picassos, Modiglianis, and de Chiricos regularly from the dealer Paul Guillaume.

The collection is often summed up by its stats: It's valued at some $25 billion and contains 181 Renoirs, 69 Cézannes, and so on. Some of its most important works are Cézanne's *The Card Players*, van Gogh's *The Postman (Joseph-Étienne Roulin)*, Seurat's *Models*, and Picasso's *Acrobat and Young Harlequin*. There is also a 45-foot triptych by Matisse commissioned for the old building and reinstalled, somewhat awkwardly, here.

The collection is also known for its eccentricity, and the odd order of things is largely re-created in the space: All those van Goghs, Renoirs, and Seurats are mixed with random folk art, Dutch landscapes, and older altar pieces. It's like the new contextualism curators are using so well at the Museum of Fine Arts, Boston, but slightly unhinged.

The new location makes the collection easier to get to, but the entry fees are steep—though there is no doubt, it's worth it.

NEARBY: Though the Rodin Museum (2151 Benjamin Franklin Parkway) is on the same campus property as the Barnes, a more unexpected side trip would be to see the Mütter Museum of the College of Physicians of Philadelphia (19 South 22nd Street)—a medical museum with specimens, instruments, and a vast collection of photography dating back to the Civil War.

INSTALLATION VIEW OF SELECTED WORKS
FROM THE PERMANENT COLLECTION,
THE BARNES FOUNDATION, PHILADELPHIA, PA.
© 2018 THE BARNES FOUNDATION

Wyeth Studios

**BRANDYWINE RIVER MUSEUM
OF ART**

1 HOFFMAN'S MILL ROAD
CHADDS FORD, PA 19317

N. C. Wyeth purchased the land and built his house in 1911 with money he made from illustrating Robert Louis Stevenson's *Treasure Island*. It's on the site of the Battle of Brandywine, the 1777 Colonial loss that found General Pulaski helping George Washington escape, and led to the fall of Philadelphia. It's fitting: Wyeth learned to paint and draw from Howard Pyle, the illustrator who promoted intense historical research, including costumes and props, as key. Unlike some historic artists' houses and studios that seem to strive to be forward-thinking, Wyeth's is a bit of a historical folly, with a massive Palladian window lighting the studio and dark-wood rooms packed with art and objects like ship models and antique firearms. The tables with his original artist's materials are a treat to see, as is the mural he painted tracing the arc of his own life.

The house was the family seat for the Wyeths, including many who became painters—son Andrew, daughters Henrietta and Carolyn, and grandson Jamie—and was a hub for creative people of all kinds, including frequent visitors F. Scott Fitzgerald, Mary Pickford, and Lillian Gish. After having painted so many Western and maritime scenes on the way to getting famous, Wyeth took to illustrating rural farm life by studying the Kuerner Farm next door. He explored many styles of painting, influenced first by the local Impressionists—the New Hope Group—and later rising American regionalists like Thomas Hart Benton, but he never made paintings that were as successful as his illustrations.

Andrew was frail as a child and grew up very close to his father, learning art from him from an early age. He stuck with a realist, regionalist style in the vein of Winslow Homer or Thomas Eakins throughout his life, always painting places and people close at hand to the family homes in Pennsylvania and Maine. His work took on a marked melancholic tone after his father's death in a car crash in 1945, and he soon became one of the most well-known American painters of all, after showing *Christina's World* in 1948. (The painting is now at the Museum of Modern Art, p. 56; and you can visit the Olson House where it was conceived in Maine.)

Like his father, he began using the neighbors as a subject and painted many pictures of Anna and Karl Kuerner. In 1971, though, he began the series of paintings that would make him infamous and inspire an early example of the "blockbuster" museum-show tour in the 1980s. He painted 45 major paintings of Helga Testorf, a married caregiver who lived on the farm. That he kept the paintings (many are nudes, disarming in their bluntness and honesty) secret from everyone including his wife and Helga's husband, only added to the excitement when they became public. Andrew's work was polarizing, in part because of the great wealth he was able to amass. The art historian Robert Rosenblum tagged him as simultaneously the most overrated and underrated American artist, but he's in most major museum collections one way or another (and since he was frequently mentioned in Charles Schultz's *Peanuts* comic strip, he can't be all bad).

You can tour Andrew's studio, as well, and the materials are even fresher feeling, more vital. You can also tour the Kuerner Farm where docents will point out famous sites of paintings, especially the ones of Helga in the stable.

Tours of the studios and the farm are organized by Brandywine River Museum of Art nearby, and before you set off on the tours, you can see major works by all 3 Wyeths—including the best collection of Andrew's work and many "Helgas"—at the museum. The Brandywine also has a strong collection of paintings by Horace Pippin, the self-taught African American artist who went on to study at the Barnes Foundation (p. 83) after receiving the attention of critics and collectors, including N. C. Wyeth. It also has a couple of major works by trompe l'oeil still-life painter George Cope and historical paintings by Howard Pyle.

ANDREW WYETH'S STUDIO AT
CHADDS FORD, PA.

PHOTO: CARLOS ALEJANDRO

The Battle of Gettysburg Cyclorama

1195 BALTIMORE PIKE
GETTYSBURG, PA 17325

Interest in the 19th-century cyclorama painting format was recently revived by excitement over contemporary artist Mark Bradford's site-specific 2018 installation *Pickett's Charge* at the Hirshhorn Museum in Washington, D.C. Here in Gettysburg, not far from the actual site of the key Civil War battle, sits one of the finest surviving examples of what was an immersive experience like nothing else at the time: Before film, 3D, IMAX, and virtual reality, cycloramas were 360-degree paintings in which a viewer could lose themselves.

Like good summer blockbuster films, cycloramas almost always depicted epic battles. Paul Philippoteaux learned the medium in Paris, where he and his father then took on the Russo-Turkish War, the Franco-Prussian War, and the Ottoman-Persian War. A Chicago businessman commissioned him to do the Battle of Gettysburg, and Philippoteaux began researching it extensively.

The 1863 battle is considered by some to have been the Civil War's decisive moment—and was the farthest north Lee's Confederate troops marched. The painting depicts the third day of the battle, known as Pickett's Charge, in which 12,500 Confederates went up against the Union line and were repulsed, with at least half dying. Philippoteaux interviewed many of the veterans of the battle, and when he was done painting a year and a half later, many praised the accuracy and emotions of the work. It was 400 feet long, 50 feet tall, and weighed 6 tons. It made so much money when it was displayed in Chicago that a second was commissioned for Boston, then one for Philadelphia, and one for Brooklyn.

Only the Boston one remains (though the whereabouts of the Brooklyn edition is unknown) and, after being discovered abandoned in a warehouse, was moved to the Gettysburg site in 1913 where numerous 50th anniversary celebrations and reunions were held. In 1965, it moved to a handsome, custom-fit building by Los Angeles modernist Richard Neutra until around 2010, when it was moved to a new building away from the "hallowed ground" of the battlefield. Sadly, the Neutra building was torn down in 2013. The latest restoration added back 14 feet of sky that had been cut away for one of the installations, and replaced a few dozen feet of diorama between the viewer and the painting.

The Battle of Gettysburg is thought to be the best of this niche of history painting. Politically, it has been criticized for showing valor on both sides with no judgement or sign of the underlying causes for the war, thus fostering the southern myth that it could have won, and may rise again.

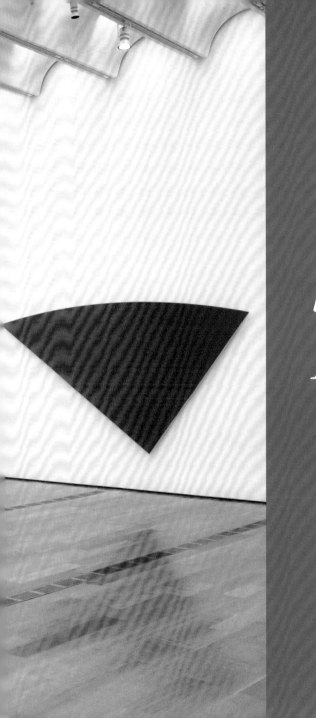

South Atlantic

Baltimore Museum of Art

10 ART MUSEUM DRIVE
BALTIMORE, MD 21218

Two sisters visited childhood friend Gertrude Stein in Paris in 1905, got introduced to Pablo Picasso, and wound up creating one of the greatest collections of modern French art in the world. Older sister Etta Cone bought Pablo Picasso and Henri Matisse drawings on the cheap that Stein and her companion, Alice B. Toklas, would flip to help support their salon. Younger sister Claribel was bolder—much bolder—pursuing big paintings over the years and managing to acquire Picasso's *Mother and Child*, Paul Cézanne's *Mont Sainte-Victoire Seen from the Bibémus Quarry*, and the largest and best collection of Matisses in the world, numbering 500 items, including *Blue Nude* and *Reclining Nude*.

The sisters gave their collection to the Baltimore Museum of Art—a Roman temple–style building opened in 1927 known for beginning to complement its collection of the usual American painting suspects with African American artists as early as 1939, including work from Joshua Johnson, Jacob Lawrence, Horace Pippin, Henry Ossawa Tanner, and sculptor Edmonia Lewis.

In the vein of all major encyclopedic museums, the BMA has holdings from all over the world—it has its Rembrandt and its Titian, it has a robust collection of African art (the *Great Mother Headdress* from Guinea's Baga region is considered the single best example of its kind). It's strong on Tang dynasty pieces and Polynesian work. One of its most important new world collections is the ceramics from Western Mexico.

In 2012, the museum opened its new wing, reimagining all of its collection in a loose style that mixed mediums and eras in friendly, informative ways. Sarah Oppenheimer was commissioned to do a site-specific work—her first for a major institution—that cut holes between the floor and walls of the new wing, creating surprising views (some via periscope), further intermingling the parts of the collection. This commission is a good example of the BMA's adventurous collecting in contemporary art—a fitting tribute to the Cone sisters' love of the new—that includes work by Olafur Eliasson, Sarah Sze, and Rirkrit Tiravanija.

NEARBY: The Walters (600 North Charles Street), as it is known, is a museum-in-a-mansion with global collections spanning thousands of years. We've seen a few famous collections in this book whose founders bought directly from artists around Paris in the early 20th century. William Walters did the same 60 years earlier, buying Géricaults, Delacroixs, Barbizon masters, and a few Impressionists, too.

INSTALLATION VIEW, BALTIMORE MUSEUM OF ART, BALTIMORE, MD.

PHOTO: RON SOLOMON

American Visionary Art Museum

800 KEY HIGHWAY
BALTIMORE, MD 21230

"It's pretty un-museumy," says Rebecca Alban Hoffberger, who founded this celebration of Outsider Art after working with psychiatric patients and a visit to Jean Dubuffet's Collection de l'Art Brut in Lausanne, Switzerland. The museum has made it a point to reject the art world's standards even within the world of self-taught and folk art, so the museum is full of the superstars in this field—Thornton Dial Jr., Reverend Howard Finster, Eugene von Bruenchenhein, Martin Ramírez, Judith Scott, Adolf Wölfli, and the whirligigs of Vollis Simpson. But it displays them side by side in annual group shows tackling universal themes with lesser-known names and new discoveries. The spaces and displays and typography on the walls tend toward the wacky, but the art and the intentions are strong and pure. The museum runs numerous public programs, including the popular Kinetic Sculpture Race.

BELOW: DAVID BEST, A LEAD ARTIST FOR THE BURNING MAN FESTIVAL, WORKED WITH A HOMELESS SHELTER NEAR THE MUSEUM TO CREATE THIS ART CAR IN ONE WEEK.

PHOTO: NICK PREVAS.

OPPOSITE: THE MUSEUM'S EXTERIOR DEPICTING THE AURORA BOREALIS NIGHT SKY.

PHOTO: DAN MEYERS

Glenstone Museum

12002 GLEN ROAD
POTOMAC, MD 20854

One of the newest major museums in America, this 200-acre campus outside Washington, D.C., was founded only in 2006. Spread across the rolling hills of a former fox-hunting estate, the original building and its new expansion pavilions, set to open by the end of 2018, hold the private collection of tech billionaire Mitchell Rales and his art-historian wife, Emily Wei Rales.

Their collection spans the postwar era, and is so vast that even 240,000 square feet can't hold it. So in the original limestone building by Charles Gwathmey, yearlong shows are put together from the collection—some by theme and some single-artist shows (which have included Fischli/Weiss, Fred Sandback, and Roni Horn). Seven of the 10 new pavilions—handsome concrete structures partially embedded in the hills by Thomas Phifer—will be devoted to single artists, rotating items from the permanent collection with the advice of the artists or their estates. These include Charles Ray, Michael Heizer, On Kawara, Cy Twombly, Brice Marden, and Martin Puryear.

The 15-minute walk between the old building and the new complex is serene, due to the landscaping and the visiting policy (tickets, which are free, are timed and limited to avoid crowding). Along the way, you'll come across 3 stone buildings built by Andy Goldsworthy and his usual crew of British stonemasons. Each has a surprise inside made from clay sourced on the grounds. There's a work comprised of 2 marble reflecting pools by Felix Gonzalez-Torres, which was fabricated after the artist's death from his open-ended plans. There's an example of Richard Serra's *Torqued Spirals* called *Sylvester*, but Glenstone also commissioned a piece called *Contour*, which traces the rolling lines of the land here. Another commission is a sound piece placed in the woods by Janet Cardiff and George Bures Miller. Wrapping up the sculpture selection are colossal works by Jeff Koons, Ellsworth Kelly, and Tony Smith.

This audacious project—its total space will be half the size of the National Gallery of Art (p. 96) down the Potomac, and it will instantly stand next to private museums like the Frick, the Barnes, and the Phillips—has been questioned for everything from its founder's curatorship to their tax relief benefits. But critics like Paul Goldberger and art-world heavies like Earl A. Powell III, director of the National Gallery of Art, are on board. Even James Cuno, CEO of the Getty, calls it "serious."

National Gallery of Art

6TH & CONSTITUTION AVENUE NW
WASHINGTON, D.C. 20565

The love for Europe is strong at "the nation's museum," between its massive rotunda modeled after the Parthenon in Rome and its obsessions with Dutch and Italian masters and 19th-century Frenchmen. Such Europhilia wasn't just prewar insecurity—it was in the museum's DNA, because the whole place got its start with a donation by Andrew Mellon that included the Hermitage Museum treasures he bought from the Soviet Union around 1930: Raphael's *Alba Madonna*, Titian's *Venus with a Mirror*, and Jan van Eyck's *Annunciation*. The museum, a Neoclassical behemoth by John Russell Pope, was accepted as a gift to the American people by Franklin D. Roosevelt in 1941. Head through an underground tunnel guided by a Leo Villareal light sculpture and you're in the East Wing, I. M. Pei's 1978 puzzle in glass-and-steel triangles, where they keep the modern and contemporary art. (The baby pyramids in the plaza here presage Pei's shocking addition to the Louvre.)

Many are drawn here by the chance to see the only Leonardo da Vinci painting in a collection in the Western Hemisphere, a portrait of a very serious young woman, Ginevra de Benci. The European galleries have a staggering amount of hits, including Johannes Vermeer's *Woman Holding A Balance* and *A Lady Writing,* Jacques-Louis David's portrait of Napoleon, Giovanni Bellini's *Feast of the Gods,* Rogier van der Weyden's *Portrait of a Lady,* and a recent, brilliantly colored addition, *The Concert* by Gerard van Honthorst. A quiet treat is Jean-Siméon Chardin's *Soap Bubbles.* The Impressionist and Post-Impressionist galleries swing big with both Édouard Manet and Claude Monet, and rival self-portraits from 1889 by van Gogh and Gauguin.

The gallery doesn't actually neglect American art—it's got Thomas Cole's cycle *The Voyage of Life,* the original of John Singleton Copley's thriller *Watson and the Shark,* and plenty of Frederic Edwin Church, Winslow Homer, Mary Cassatt, John Singer Sargent, and Thomas Eakins. Over in the East Wing, you'll need to see Pablo Picasso's *Family of Saltimbanques,* Arshile Gorky's *The Artist and His Mother,* Jackson Pollock's *Number 1, 1950 (Lavender Mist)* and *Mural*—his biggest painting at 20 feet wide. There's also an entire room of Amedeo Modigliani paintings and sculptures that's revelatory—it's so rare to see him without a bunch of Cubo-Futurist cacophony surrounding him.

New spaces were opened to the public after a renovation in 2016, including single-artist galleries at the top of the towers. The Mark Rothko room makes the most of its overhead natural light. There's also a rooftop sculpture terrace where Nam June Paik's *Ugly Buddha* watches TV and Katharina Fritsch's 15-foot-tall, neon-blue rooster stands guard. (It's on long-term loan from the Glenstone Museum up the Potomac (p. 95).

Six acres of sculptures await those with any remaining energy. There's a mosaic by Marc Chagall, commissioned by John and Evelyn Nef in Georgetown. Louise Bourgeois has a spider whose creepy stance mirrors an earlier geometric creature, *Moondog,* by Tony Smith. There's playful work by Lucas Samaras, Claes Oldenburg, and Barry Flanagan; a harrowing holocaust-related work by Magdalena Abakanowicz; and a giant silver tree by Roxy Paine.

THE EAST BUILDING ATRIUM FEATURING A SCULPTURE BY ALEXANDER CALDER, THE NATIONAL GALLERY OF ART, WASHINGTON, D.C. © 2018 BOARD OF TRUSTEES, NATIONAL GALLERY OF ART, WASHINGTON

The Smithsonian Institution

600 MARYLAND AVENUE SW
WASHINGTON, D.C. 20002

The Smithsonian is one of the biggest and most successful cultural institutions on earth. Its efforts preserve history and art and design, and expand our understanding of what America means. It's impossible to cover everything it does—from the National Portrait Gallery to the Archives of American Art to outposts and affiliates in New Orleans, New York, and elsewhere. In addition to the Freer, the Hirshhorn, and the National Museum of African American History and Culture, here are a few more art stops that must be made in the Capitol.

SMITHSONIAN AMERICAN ART MUSEUM (F STREET NW & 8TH STREET NW) is as friendly and down to earth a serious art museum can be. It strives to span the entire story of the country, starting in colonial times and racing right up to the inclusion of video games as art. Along the way, it's been a pioneer in treating photography, folk art, African American art, and Latin American art on equal footing with traditional Western views of what art is. Nam June Paik's room-sized neon and video monitor piece, *Electronic Superhighway: Continental U.S., Alaska, Hawaii* sets the fun, inclusive tone here (in fact, the artist's entire archive is the anchor of the Film and New

Media department). James Hampton's *The Throne of the Third Heaven of the Nations' Millennium General Assembly* is another room-sized assembly, and considered one of the most important by an artist in the African American "yard show" tradition of the South. The 20th-century collection includes Edward Hopper's *Cape Cod Morning* and work by Jacob Lawrence, Georgia O'Keeffe, Joseph Stella, and other greats. One unusual area the museum collects more deeply than most is the Washington Color School artists of the 1950s and '60s, including work by Sam Gilliam, Thomas Downing, Paul Reed, and Gene Davis. The art by Asian Americans includes work by Yasuo Kuniyoshi, Chiura Obata, and Isamu Noguchi. In the African American section, the work ranges from the 19th-century's Joshua Johnson to Sister Gertrude Morgan to Mickalene Thomas. The decorative arts building, the Renwick, includes a Nick Cave *Soundsuit*, Wendell Castle's *Ghost Clock*, and furniture by Sam Maloof.

NATIONAL MUSEUM OF THE AMERICAN INDIAN (4TH STREET SW & INDEPENDENCE AVENUE SW) is one of the biggest collections of native arts from the Americas, spanning from Patagonia to the Arctic Circle. It covers every region with top-of-their-class objects, including beaded boots from the Shoshone people, Navajo weaving, Pueblo pottery, and exquisite carved-wood pieces from the Pacific Northwest. The museum is notable for having Native Americans in a large portion of its leadership

positions, and even its architecture team, led by Douglas Cardinal of the Blackfoot tribe in Canada, was mostly native. The museum has received some criticism: Despite the quality of the objects, the scholarship and storylines holding them together sometimes seems to be adrift. But for most, it's a way to see the best of the cultural history of these peoples in a new light.

SMITHSONIAN NATIONAL PORTRAIT GALLERY (8TH STREET NW & F STREET NW), known for its Gilbert Stuart portraits of George Washington and the other early presidents, got a fresh spotlight in 2018 when it became the home of the official portraits of Barack and Michelle Obama by Kehinde Wiley and Amy Sherald, respectively. The two painters are rising African American art stars, and their bold work stands out among the past presidential portraits. Elsewhere in the collection you can find portraits of Alexander Hamilton by John Trumbull, Henry Cabot Lodge by John Singer Sargent, Mary Cassatt by Edgar Degas, Beauford Delaney by Georgia O'Keeffe, and the best collection of Mathew Brady's Civil War photography.

NAM JUNE PAIK, *ELECTRONIC SUPERHIGHWAY: CONTINENTAL U.S., ALASKA, HAWAII,* 1995, SMITHSONIAN AMERICAN ART MUSEUM, GIFT OF THE ARTIST. © NAM JUNE PAIK ESTATE

James Abbott McNeill Whistler's *The Peacock Room*

THE FREER GALLERY OF ART
1050 INDEPENDENCE AVE SW
WASHINGTON, D.C. 20560

Money, acrimony, a love affair, and a madman who coated himself entirely in gold leaf: *The Peacock Room* comes with its own over-the-top drama. Widely regarded as the best-preserved masterpiece of the Aesthetic movement of the late 19th century, the room that American painter James Abbott McNeill Whistler called his "complete art piece"— and his client called a disaster— survived many moves and a few battles since its creation in London in 1876.

It can be hard to understand that an interior so beautiful and luxurious was intended not only as an art piece in its own right, but also as an act of rebellion. The Aesthetic movement, which counted Oscar Wilde, Dante Gabriel Rossetti, and Aubrey Beardsley among its leaders, was a reaction to Victorian England's buttoned-up tastes and incessant moralizing. Its motto was "Art for art's sake," and it was influenced by the increased access to Asian art after the lifting of trade embargoes. Art was meant to inform every aspect of life, so many forms (such as interior design) were to be elevated to the level of fine art.

Whistler, who was already known for his work's debt to the Japanese woodblock prints of Hokusai and Hiroshige, made statements indicating that the figures in his paintings were mere props to create "harmony" around: "Art should be independent of all claptrap—should stand alone and appeal to the artistic sense of eye or ear without confounding this with emotions entirely foreign to it..." he said. The idea still works, and inspires ecstatic reactions, as the *New Yorker*'s Peter Schjeldahl wrote after a visit in 2011: "It realizes a synesthetic fusion of dazzling spectacle and intimate touch, evoking music and something like a subliminal, ambrosial perfume."

The room was commissioned by shipping magnate Frederick R. Leyland to showcase Whistler's *The Princess from the Land of Porcelain*. It was a time of great fascination with Asian art in the West, and Leyland also intended to house his collection of blue-and-white Chinese porcelain in the room. Whistler was brought in by the original designer, Thomas Jekyll, to paint one panel to compliment the room, and began a turquoise-ground-and-gilt-peacock motif. In a classic case of mission creep, he soon eliminated all notes of red in the room and, when Jekyll took ill, really ran amok, painting the peacocks and harmonious decorative details everywhere. Leyland was not pleased at all, and refused to pay him. Jekyll, when he finally saw it, went home and was later found curled up on his floor covered in gold leaf, insane. Whistler and Leyland fought for many years, with Whistler tormenting Leyland with caricatures of a pompous and overbearing peacock.

(Whistler was also linked to Leyland's estranged wife.)

In 1904, Leyland's family sold it to the American railroad industry titan and Whistler collector Charles Lang Freer, who installed it in his mansion in Detroit and used it to display his own more variegated collection of Chinese porcelain. In 1923, it was installed in the Freer Collection in Washington, D.C., the first dedicated fine-arts museum built for the Smithsonian Institution. *The Peacock Room*'s example of peak Anglo Asian style makes it a fitting centerpiece for the Freer Gallery, which marries American collections—including major Winslow Homer and Childe Hassam paintings—with the largest museum and library devoted to Asian art in the United States (in conjunction with the adjoining Arthur M. Sackler Gallery).

INTERIOR VIEW OF JAMES ABBOTT MCNEILL WHISTLER, *HARMONY IN BLUE AND GOLD: THE PEACOCK ROOM*, THE FREER GALLERY OF ART AND ARTHUR M. SACKLER GALLERY, SMITHSONIAN INSTITUTION, WASHINGTON, D.C. GIFT OF CHARLES LANG FREER, F1904.61

Hirshhorn Museum and Sculpture Garden

INDEPENDENCE AVENUE SW &
7TH STREET SW
WASHINGTON, D.C. 20560

A cylinder on 4 posts, the building holding the Hirshhorn Museum has been called a giant abstract sculpture—so much so that it could be used for a game of ring toss with the Washington Monument. But the round halls are no gimmick, and the museum, designed by Gordon Bunshaft in 1966, has been praised for its logical flow. Artists have made use of the unique spaces afforded for site-specific works—most recently Mark Bradford, with his 400-foot-long *Pickett's Charge* inspired by the cyclorama painting at Gettysburg (p. 86).

The Hirshhorn was conceived in the 1930s to be a modern art museum, in contrast to the emphasis on Old Masters at the National Gallery (p. 96). It did a good job: It's got Pablo Picasso, Henri Matisse, Mary Cassatt, Edward Hopper, and Francis Bacon. It's got the New York School with Mark Rothko, Jackson Pollock, and Willem de Kooning. And it's got the Minimalists, color field, and more. Its 4-acre sculpture garden has a Jeff Koons, a David Smith, an Alexander Calder, and Auguste Rodin's powerful *The Burghers of Calais*. It also has a "Wishing Tree" by Yoko Ono—which lets visitors write their wishes and attach them.

EXTERIOR VIEW OF THE HIRSHHORN MUSEUM AND SCULPTURE GARDEN, SMITHSONIAN INSTITUTION, WASHINGTON, D.C.
PHOTO: CATHY CARVER

National Museum of African American History and Culture

1400 CONSTITUTION AVENUE NW
WASHINGTON, D.C. 20560

A wonderful moment at the end of Barack Obama's presidency was the opening of this museum in 2016. The striking building in the shape of an upside down ziggurat—the best new building in Washington, D.C. in decades—was designed by Ghanian British architect David Adjaye to look like a Yoruban crown. The museum had been an idea going all the way back to World War I, when African American soldiers returning from Europe first raised the idea of a museum honoring their experience. Like many museums in the Smithsonian group, the National Museum of African American History and Culture seeks to document many facets of American life, so there's quite a bit of history here, including objects from a sunken slave ship, Harriet Tubman's belongings, an entire Jim Crow–era railway car, and Chuck Berry's red Cadillac.

But the art doesn't disappoint, with both early modernists and artists such as Hale Woodruff, Thornton Dial, Beauford Delaney, Romare Bearden, Purvis Young, Jacob Lawrence, Clementine Hunter, Archibald Motley, Lois Mailou Jones, and Henry Ossawa Tanner. More contemporary artists include Amy Sherald (who is responsible for the universally acclaimed official portrait of Michelle Obama unveiled in 2018), Whitfield Lovell, and Chakaia Booker. Some items that fit both camps work—ever since the Souls Grown Deep Foundation toured *The Quilts of Gee's Bend*, they've been heralded for their sophisticated abstract compositions and use of color. Another is the *Mothership*—a stage prop designed by funk superstar George Clinton and used at Parliament-Funkadelic concerts. It's exuberant Pop sculpture at its best.

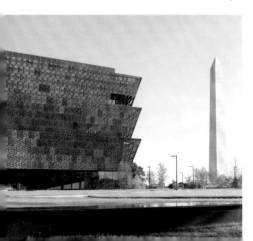

LEFT: EXTERIOR VIEW OF THE NATIONAL MUSEUM OF AFRICAN AMERICAN HISTORY AND CULTURE, WASHINGTON, D.C.
PHOTO: MICHAEL VENTURA/ALAMY STOCK PHOTO.

RIGHT: INSTALLATION VIEW OF *VISUAL ART AND THE AMERICAN IMAGINATION*, NATIONAL MUSEUM OF AFRICAN AMERICAN HISTORY AND CULTURE, WASHINGTON, D.C.
PHOTO: ALAN KARCHMER/NMAAHC.

IN THIS TEMPLE
AS IN THE HEARTS OF THE PEOPLE
FOR WHOM HE SAVED THE UNION
THE MEMORY OF ABRAHAM LINCOLN
IS ENSHRINED FOREVER

QUIET
RESPECT
PLEASE

41

Lincoln Memorial

2 LINCOLN MEMORIAL CIRCLE NW
WASHINGTON, D.C. 20037

VIETNAM VETERANS MEMORIAL
5 HENRY BACON DRIVE NW
WASHINGTON, D.C. 20245

It took until 1922 to create a fitting tribute to Abraham Lincoln—America's greatest president. The 19-foot-tall seated portrait by Daniel Chester French shows Lincoln in contemplation—taking stock, perhaps, of the Civil War and its costs. Despite sitting in a Greek temple built by Henry Bacon, this Lincoln is a man, not a god. We can see it by his loosened tie, his rumbled hair, the nervous tension as his fingers grip the armrests of his chair. It's not the triumphant obelisk of the Washington Monument, and it's no hero on horseback.

French was one of a handful of superstar sculptors of his era. Maybe it was because Walt Whitman was a family friend, or Ralph Waldo Emerson sat for his bust, but French brought out psychological elements in his subjects that other neoclassical sculptors missed. His Lincoln shows anguish, imperfections, worry. It's how we like to see him.

Nearby on the mall is the Vietnam Veterans Memorial—another innovation in grieving and memory—designed by architect and artist Maya Lin. Its two 296-foot-long walls taper from 10 feet tall to 8 inches tall. The names of fallen soldiers are etched into black granite polished so that the viewer's reflection stares back at them.

It was stunning at the time (some vets groups were so upset, they pushed for a traditional bronze by Frederick Hart of 3 soldiers walking together, fatigued, as if back from combat), and it's still always moving. The memorial launched Lin's career, and her work can be seen globally, including at Storm King Art Center (p. 45), the campus of Yale University, and the Civil Rights Memorial in Montgomery, Alabama, in front of the Southern Poverty Law Center.

LINCOLN MEMORIAL,
WASHINGTON, D.C.

PHOTO: CAROL M. HIGHSMITH ARCHIVE,
LIBRARY OF CONGRESS, PRINTS AND
PHOTOGRAPHS DIVISION

Virginia Museum of Fine Arts

200 NORTH BOULEVARD
RICHMOND, VA 23220

A world-class collection of Fabergé eggs (the Stradivarius of the Easter decoration world) is an oddball main event for a major art museum. To some, it's gaudy and silly-seeming. But the major collection of 47 of Russian jeweler Peter Carl Fabergé's jeweled baubles here (originally bought by Lillian Pratt with her Lord & Taylor charge account) speaks to a mindset with a high respect for decorative arts and design—they're not lesser beings than the paintings on the wall.

The Virginia Museum of Fine Arts opened its Georgian Revival building in 1936 and began to grow very quickly after the donation of the eggs in the 1940s. It received the Lewis Family collection of Art Nouveau work, spanning all art forms and countries taken up with the fever in the early 19th century, including wonderful Vienna Secession work; Arts and Crafts work by Greene & Greene, Charles Rennie Mackintosh, and Gustav Stickley; and Parisian great Eileen Gray.

The museum was always innovative, thanks to its first director, Leslie Cheek Jr., who embellished displays of Egyptian funerary art with theatrical, over-the-top lighting treatments, started the first ever night hours at an American museum, and created, in 1953, the first Artmobile—a big truck full of art used for outreach in the countryside. He also built a theater—one of the first times visual and performing arts had been put together in an institution like this.

The museum grew, through many additions, into the kind of encyclopedic temple to art every big, East Coast city has to have. Its African collection covers the Kuba, Akan, Yoruba, and Kongo peoples especially well. The Asian collection has 800 prints by master Kawase Hasui. There are Goyas, Murillos, and Poussins, plus a Delacroix and one of Artemisia Gentileschi's greatest paintings, *Venus and Cupid.*

The modern collection has the distinction of having been acquired by its collectors by trading electronic goods to artists when they started in the 1950s and '60s—they were the founders of Best Buy. Work included Helen Frankenthaler, Jasper Johns, Robert Rauschenberg, and Lee Bontecou. The German Expressionism collection was given by the Fisher family after they fled Germany in 1934, and includes top Emile Noldes and Ernst Ludwig Kirchners. More contemporary work includes painting by Kehinde Wiley, Julie Mehretu, Mickalene Thomas, and Theaster Gates.

NEARBY: An hour-and-a-half away in Norfolk is the Chrysler Museum of Art (1 Memorial Place), the brainchild of the son of the founder of Chrysler Motors, who began buying directly from artists in Paris. It's got a bit of everything, including Gian Lorenzo Bernini's last piece, Paul Gauguin's mysterious *The Loss of Virginity*, and some Renoirs and Cassatts. Things get fun in the contemporary galleries with a monumental mixed-media protest piece by Jaune Quick-to-See Smith, a painting by Barkley Hendricks, and Nam June Paik's hilarious *Hamlet Robot.* The museum is known best for its glass collection, anchored by plenty of Tiffany, and a glass-blowing studio where the public can try their hand at the art.

AMERICAN ART GALLERIES, VIRGINIA MUSEUM OF FINE ARTS, RICHMOND, VA.

PHOTO (DETAIL): DAVID STOVER © VIRGINIA MUSEUM OF FINE ARTS

Black Mountain College Museum and Arts Center

120 COLLEGE STREET
ASHEVILLE, NC 28801

This legendary, free-spirited art school petered out after World War II, but it influenced such a broad swath of American arts and letters that it has become a legend. Founded in the late 1920s by John Andrew Rice and Theodore Dreier as an alternative to almost everything, they distilled ideas on teaching from the Bauhaus (and some joined in from Weimar, including Walter Gropius, who consulted on the main building, and Josef and Anni Albers, who taught). The school would go on to produce John Cage, Merce Cunningham, Ruth Asawa, Cy Twombly, Frank O'Hara, Charles Olson, Robert Rauschenberg, M. C. Richards, Peter Voulkos, and many more.

Black Mountain College Museum and Arts Center displays paintings and sculptures by some of the lesser-known names among teachers and graduates, but includes many fine ceramics by Richards, and early sculptures by Asawa. It also has copious artifacts, from signage to art-show fliers to course syllabi. The Black Mountain College Foundation also runs the school's original poetry press, the *Jargon Society*, from here, and an organization called DEATH that incubates artistic projects and puts on

shows of contemporary art sympathetic with the Black Mountain vibe.

The museum also occasionally organizes special events at the school's original site 15 miles east of Asheville toward the mountains. You can see the mix of International Style architecture with vernacular barns and woodwork, and the staff will tell you about some of the proto-happenings on the spots they occurred. Efforts are being made to restore a set of frescoes by José Mariano de Creeft on the support pylons holding up the Bauhaus-like Studies Building. The Christian boys' camp on the site now is wary of people dropping by. So plan ahead with the museum or, better yet, come during the annual Lake Eden Arts Festival in the first half of May and you'll have the run of the place.

NEARBY: Another school with a distinguished history is the Penland School of Crafts (67 Doras Trail, Bakersville), about 50 miles away. Beginning in 1923, weaving, ceramics, and work in other mediums has been taught in distinctive log-cabin studios. Anni Albers spent some time teaching here, and you can drop by resident artists' studios or take a tour every Wednesday.

INSTALLATION VIEW OF SELECTED WORKS FROM THE PERMANENT COLLECTION, INCLUDING ROBERT RAUSCHENBERG, RUTH ASAWA, SUSAN WEIL, M.C. RICHARDS, DAVID WEINRIB, AND JOSEPH FIORE, BLACK MOUNTAIN COLLEGE MUSEUM AND ARTS CENTER, ASHEVILLE, NC.

PHOTO: MICHAEL OPPENHEIM PHOTOGRAPHY

44

Paradise Garden

200 NORTH LEWIS STREET
SUMMERVILLE, GA 30747

The work of the Reverend Howard Finster, Paradise Garden, was almost lost to the kudzu—an invasive vine in the South—after his death in 2001. Decades of work using broken bicycle parts, shards of mirrors, soda bottles, and car parts to create what started as a roadside attraction and became a 4-acre spiritual mission, have been excavated and restored since 2012. It's surprising things got so bad, since Finster had become both a member of the Outsider Art world and a pop-culture phenomenon by the 1980s. Talking Heads and R.E.M. used his paintings, with their Bible-based rants written all over them, on record covers, and there were porch parties where everyone from the B-52s to Keith Haring visited. Finster's work was in the collections of the Smithsonian Institution, the Philadelphia Museum of Art, and Atlanta's High Museum.

It's a shambles still, but while the restorers know they'll never make it the pristine, colorful heaven Finster created, they do believe they're bringing back the spirit of the place. They've saved the Mirror House, Bottle House, Mosaic Garden, Rolling Chair Gallery, Hubcap Tower, and the 5-story World's Folk Art Chapel with its 12-sided balcony. It's easygoing here; the staff is friendly. You can even stay over in the on-site Airbnb apartment.

Finster is still a superstar in the Outsider Art scene, and with some 46,000 pieces of artwork out there, there's plenty to go around. The American Visionary Art Museum in Baltimore (p. 92) calls him "America's most prolific self-tutored and 'on fire' artist."

HOWARD FINSTER'S PARADISE GARDEN, SUMMERVILLE, GA.

PHOTO: DEBORAH GRAY MITCHELL

High Museum of Art

1280 PEACHTREE STREET NE
ATLANTA, GA 30309

Not many museums like this—grand institutions that are cultural pillars of major U.S. cities—have focused as much on African American art, and African American visitors, as the High Museum. By the end of 2017, it announced that its marketing and programming efforts had raised the visitorship to over 50 percent nonwhite, and that over half of its shows were devoted to people of color, women, or LGBT artists.

The museum got its start in 1905 in a mock Tudor house. After several moves, it built a Richard Meier building in 1983 that was regarded as good-looking but kind of useless for showing art. Renzo Piano, of Centre Georges Pompidou and Menil Collection fame, was brought in in 2005, and the High finally had a world-class museum space, with 1,000 "scoops" in the roof filtering in natural light.

The collections don't try to do everything, but they do plenty. Areas of collecting include photography (with a trove of Civil Rights–era photography) and the strongest U.S. collections of Eugène Atget, Harry Callahan, and Abelardo Morell. Then there are decorative arts (with ceramicists Peter Voulkos and Viola Frey, as well as icons like Frank Lloyd Wright and Ettore Sottsass) and European work

including Giovanni Bellini and Vittore Carpaccio, as well as tons of Edgar Degas, Henri de Toulouse-Lautrec, and some beautiful Édouard Vuillard. There are too many great American paintings to begin to list.

The High's approach to African art includes masterpieces from Burkina Faso, Central Africa, and the Yoruba people, as well as contemporary artists such as El Anatsui and Malick Sidibe. It makes an effort to span the African diaspora and connect these cultures to African Americans.

The contemporary collection is strong on African Americans, too, with work from Jean-Michel Basquiat, Kara Walker, Faith Ringgold, David Hammons, Robert Colescott, Fred Wilson, Chakala Booker, Betye Saar, Lorna Simpson, and Nick Cave. (It also includes people like Alex Katz, Alfredo Jaar, Anish Kapoor, KAWS, Julie Mehretu, Judy Pfaff, and Sarah Sze.)

The diversity efforts weren't a new, inorganic add on. The High had been collecting work by self-taught black artists from the South for decades. But it got a big shot in the arm in the spring of 2017 when it was given 54 pieces from the Souls Grown Deep Foundation—a group that promotes African American art of the South. It included 11 quilts from Gee's Bend and paintings by Lonnie Holley and Ronald Lockett, as well as 13 Thornton Dial paintings to add to what is already the biggest collection of his work.

More self-taught art at the High includes the biggest collections of Bill Traylor and Nellie Mae Rowe, as well as Reverend Howard Finster, creator

of Paradise Garden (p. 112). Many are "yard artists" like Finster, and the High has re-created some environments to give context to the work of Purvis Young, Mary T. Smith, and James Harold Jennings.

NEARBY: In Piedmont Park (1320 Monroe Drive NE), there's a children's playground from 1977 designed by Isamu Noguchi. To be honest, it doesn't look that fun for kids—but it's great for design types to geek out on. Also in the park is David Hammons's tribute to Nelson Mandela, complete with jail cell bars. Harlem Renaissance star Elizabeth Catlett created a bronze relief sculpture at City Hall, and Thornton Dial's tribute to Congressman John Lewis made of found objects is in Freedom Park. There's also a controversial Sol LeWitt piece in the Fourth Ward called 54 Columns—apparently some locals think it looks like an unfinished freeway overpass, support columns only.

ROBINSON ATRIUM RAMP AND SKYLIGHTS, HIGH MUSEUM OF ART, ATLANTA, GA.

The Dalí Museum

1 DALÍ BOULEVARD
ST. PETERSBURG, FL 33701

A major tourist destination on the water in St. Petersburg, Florida, the Dalí crams them in through its bulbous glass entrance called the "Enigma." The fact that you enter, rather than exit, through the gift shop, with its avalanche of cheap Salvador Dalí kitsch, might be a deal breaker for some. But the museum's backstory is endearing, and makes you want to give it a chance.

The museum is born of Reynolds and Eleanor Morse, an Ohio couple who bought Dalí's *Daddy Longlegs of the Evening-Hope!* in 1942 and, after meeting him at a party in New York City a year later, struck up a friendship that lasted 4 decades. Eventually, their collection outgrew their living room, and crowds overwhelmed the small museum they built nearby (where Dalí presided over the opening in 1971). After that, crowds swarmed the warehouse the Morses opened in 1982 in St. Petersburg. The new building—by architects HOK, of the National Air and Space Museum in D.C.—fits the roughly half million or so who visit each year.

The dripping watches on the park benches out front are a little Disney, but the art inside is for real. The collection has 7 of Dalí's 18 major works, including *The Hallucinogenic Toreador* and *The Discovery of America*

by Christopher Columbus. It also has the most work by the artist outside of Europe. The objects inside—the *Aphrodisiac Telephone* (with its lobster handset), the bronze chess set made in honor of Marcel Duchamp, and the outrageous *Venus de Milo with Drawers (and Pom Poms)*—are more fun than the paintings (and were arguably more influential).

To its credit, the gift shop does have an homage to Dalí's *Rainy Taxi*: a 1930s Rolls-Royce. Drop a coin in the slot and you'll set off a rainstorm inside.

NEARBY: The University of South Florida across the bay in Tampa is the home of Graphicstudio (3702 Spectrum Blvd #100, Tampa)—a printmaking studio that has had thousands of visiting artists. You can take a tour and see where artists as varied as Robert Rauschenberg, Alice Aycock, Judy Chicago, Keith Sonnier, and John Waters have worked. Also on campus is the USF Contemporary Art Museum, where work from the Graphicstudio visiting artists is at the core of the collection.

SALVADOR DALÍ, *THE HALLUCINOGENIC TOREADOR*, 1969–70, OIL ON CANVAS. © SALVADOR DALÍ. FUNDACÍON GALA-SALVADOR DALÍ (ARTIST RIGHTS SOCIETY), 2017 / COLLECTION OF THE SALVADOR DALÍ MUSEUM, INC., ST. PETERSBURG, FL, 2017. © 2018 – SALVADOR DALÍ MUSEUM, INC., ST. PETERSBURG, FL.

47

The John and Mabel Ringling Museum of Art

5401 BAY SHORE ROAD
SARASOTA, FL 34243

Built by circus royalty in the 1930s, the Ringling Museum truly feels like a palace. Its pink Spanish Revival arms stretch out toward the Gulf of Mexico, surrounding formal gardens. Its galleries are actually big enough to display its collection of gargantuan Peter Paul Rubens paintings, like *The Meeting of Abraham and Melchizedek*. The 66-acre summer estate of the billionaire family, with its Venetian-style mansion called the Ca d'Zan, is the Hearst Castle moment here: It's all about ogling the spectacular riches. But the museum is the real deal—it contains work from all eras and all continents, and its European and American painting collections matter. There's Diego Velázquez, Paolo Veronese, Giovanni Bellini, Nicolas Poussin, and more. And there's enough work to put on interesting rotating exhibitions and to lend to other touring shows. It also has a 3,000-square-foot James Turrell "Skyspace" called *Joseph's Coat*, which is an excellent way to enjoy the Gulf light.

INSTALLATION VIEW OF THE JOHN & MABLE RINGLING MUSEUM OF ART, SARASOTA, FL.

PHOTO: COURTESY THE JOHN & MABLE RINGLING MUSEUM OF ART

48

Pérez Art Museum Miami

1103 BISCAYNE BOULEVARD
MIAMI, FL 33132

For once the superstar architects brought in to take a museum to the next level—in this case, the Swiss duo Herzog & de Meuron—actually seem to have looked around town a bit before they started sketching. Unlike dozens of wannabe Bilbao's plopped down like UFOs in cities across the country, the 2012 building for the Pérez Art Museum in downtown Miami plays with vernacular architecture and tropical lushness in a way that allows for a wonderful experience for visitors. The flow of the museum has been praised by major critics, and artists love it. Once you hear the inspiration for the collection of tall, concrete pylons surrounding the building and its irregular, raft-like overhangs, you'll appreciate that they had art at heart when they designed it: It's based on Stiltsville, the famous ragtag neighborhood of houses sitting out in the Atlantic off the coast here.

The public spaces flow indoors and out and make for great parties (during the big art week in December, the parties can swell to almost 5,000 people). But the Pérez distinguishes itself in its art as well; focused on modern and contemporary work, it really does feel like it's leaning forward instead of looking over its shoulder. Experiments with virtual reality, hanging vines by French botanist/artist Patrice Blanc, and items in the permanent collection by Olafur Eliasson, Ernesto Neto, and Konstantin Grcic, reinforce this notion.

Cuban art is in the DNA of this museum, which was founded in 1983, and in its billionaire namesake, Jorge Pérez, the real-estate developer who helped fund the new building, has made sure the museum has the best collection of Cuban art in the United States, having given several batches of major works that have fueled a series of shows. Highlights of the Cuban collection include work by Wifredo Lam, Hernan Bas, Los Carpinteros, Amelia Peláez, Mario Carreño, and José Bedia Valdés. Pérez also donated work by other Latin American artists, including Diego Rivera, Damián Ortega, and Beatriz González.

There's been controversy about Pérez and the naming rights—some directors resigned over it. But billionaire pissing matches are a very Miami thing, and so it's another way the Pérez Art Museum is perfectly of its place and time.

NEARBY: Across the causeway in South Beach is the Wolfsonian Museum (1001 Washington Avenue), run by Florida International University. It's got archives of objects, machines, and printed matter, and puts together innovative shows, like an ongoing exhibition that looks at Depression-era public works and their attempts to address race issues. It also has a permanent site-specific installation by Lawrence Weiner.

HANGING GARDENS ON THE EXTERIOR
OF PÉREZ ART MUSEUM, MIAMI, FL.

PHOTO: ROBIN HILL © 2018

The Private Collections of Miami

MIAMI, FL

Miami is many things: a gateway to the Caribbean, home to vibrant Cuban and Haitian cultures in the U.S., and the site of America's biggest art fair, Art Basel Miami Beach. The city also excels at conspicuous consumption—it's the place in America where the billionaires—and those within shouting distance of that status—show off their art purchases like nowhere else.

The Rubell Family Collection, which started in New York in 1964 but got the ball rolling when it opened to the public in Miami in 1993, is the best known. And it became the model, with its smart warehouse spaces, adventurous collecting, special projects, and great parties. Now there are a bunch of these single-collection museums. They may not be as elaborate monuments to ego as Eli Broad's Broad Museum in L.A., but they compete like crazy and heighten the drama in the Miami art scene. Though all trot out their best efforts that heady first week of December during Miami Art week, they're open year round.

A. RUBELL FAMILY COLLECTION (95 NW 29TH STREET, MIAMI, FL 33127) Forty-thousand square feet and the one to beat. It could give many institutes of contemporary art a run for their money. Group shows the Rubell has curated from its collection have traveled to the Detroit Institute of Arts, the Corcoran in Washington, D.C., and many more museums. The collection is known for its strong holdings in the work of Jean-Michel Basquiat, Keith Haring, Jeff Koons, Cady Noland, Yayoi Kusama, Cindy Sherman, and Kara Walker; but Mera and Don Rubell are also known for aggressively seeking out new talent. Bonus points for opening their galleries in a former Drug Enforcement Agency facility to give a little *Miami Vice* thrill.

B. THE MARGULIES COLLECTION AT THE WAREHOUSE (591 NW 27TH STREET, MIAMI, FL 33127) Real-estate developer Martin Margulies's first love is sculpture, and at the core of his collection, in another 45,000-square-foot space, are pieces by Donald Judd,

George Segal, Willem de Kooning, Antony Gormley, and Sol LeWitt. The collection dates back to a Coconut Grove sculpture garden Margulies ran that eventually had to move, and opened in the current space in 1999. The space is a natural for site-specific commissions like *Your now is my surroundings* by Olafur Eliasson, for which you go up a flight of outdoor stairs and into a tall, narrow hall of mirrors open to the sky. Many works are giant productions to bring out and install, so keep an eye out for annual shows with pieces like Do Ho Suh's cloth re-creation of the New York hallway he first lived in in art school.

Margulies only began collecting photography in 1992—his first photo was a large piece by Thomas Ruff—but at the heart of it is an even more personal vision than the contemporary art he collects. He grew up the son of grocers in New York in the 1940s, and has acquired contemporaneous work by Helen Levitt and simpatico photographers Dorothea Lange and Lewis Hine. Not quite a Rosebud moment, but it can thaw out your skepticism about mega-rich collectors to hear things like this.

C. CRAIG ROBINS COLLECTION (3841 NE 2ND AVENUE, MIAMI, FL 33137) Craig Robins is another real-estate developer who did very, very well in Miami and is credited with reviving the neighborhood now known as the Design District. He also founded Design Miami, to coincide with Art Basel each year, which has become one of the most important design events in America.

The first art piece he ever bought, as a student in Barcelona, was a Salvador Dalí, but the collection is known now for its mix of art, architecture, and design. Chief in the art category are some very design-friendly artists, like Richard Tuttle and John Baldessari. Paul McCarthy, Mike Kelley, Marlene Dumas, and Nicole Eisenman are also represented. In the design and architecture mode, there's work by Gio Ponti, Jean Prouvé, the Campana Brothers, Ron Arad, and Zaha Hadid. Visits are by appointment, and free on weekdays.

Nearby in the Design District, there are a pair of massive murals by John Baldessari on a parking garage (printed on perforated metal), a recent piece by Urs Fischer of a delinquent skeleton passed out like a wino

at a bus stop, and one of Buckminster Fuller's *Fly's Eye Domes*. If you make the trip to Aqua, Robins's development on Alison Island, you can see a mural by Tuttle—his first ever public commission—and sculptures by Guillermo Kuitca and local Miami hero Mark Handforth.

D. DE LA CRUZ COLLECTION (23 NE 41ST STREET, MIAMI, FL 33137) The private collection of Rosa and Carlos de la Cruz is free, and the couple even lets the public view their collection in their home by appointment. The Cuban American pair are known for ambitious commissions, for their project space, and also for strong holdings by Cuban-born artists like Felix Gonzalez-Torres and Ana Mendieta. Others in the collection include Isa Genzken, Christopher Wool, Mark Bradford, Allora & Calzadilla, and Peter Doig, making it a distinctive point of view.

PAGES 122–23: SELECTED WORKS BY KEITH HARING AT THE RUBELL FAMILY COLLECTION, MIAMI, FL.

OPPOSITE: INSTALLATION VIEW OF THE DE LA CRUZ COLLECTION, MIAMI, FL.

Midwest

Diego Rivera's *Detroit Industry* and Detroit Institute of Arts

5200 WOODWARD AVENUE
DETROIT, MI 48202

Mass production never looked so good as in the Mexican painter's best mural in the United States, *Detroit Industry*, commissioned by Edsel Ford. The massive mural is the heart of the Detroit Institute of Arts, which also boasts an encyclopedic collection spanning ancient Egypt to the current day, housed in a grand 1923 Beaux-Arts Italian Renaissance building.

Not one to improvise, Rivera spent months in 1932 soaking in the grand efficiency of the Ford Motor Plant. He was in awe of the machinery, and where you might think that the man who painted farmers, laborers, and revolutionaries would frown upon the Motor City's capitalist triumphalism, Rivera saw the promise of freedom from proletariat drudgery in automation. He gives the Ford-factory floor incredible energy—and a giant steel-stamping machine that dominates one panel is designed to look like the pre-Hispanic creation god, Coatlicue. Other panels also treat the creative and destructive potential of the booming aviation industry. There was some controversy: In a panel about medical advancements, a baby being vaccinated surrounded by animals made the Catholic Church call for the mural's destruction. *Detroit Industry* benefits from beautiful natural light from the building's expansive skylights.

Other Rivera murals in the U.S. should not be missed—especially the 3 painted around San Francisco a year before Rivera's trip to Detroit (see San Francisco Murals, p. 225). The only other mural in the country that's better known than the one in Detroit is the infamous Rockefeller Center mural that was painted over because it included the image of Joseph Stalin.

The Detroit Institute also holds a huge collection of American paintings from John James Audubon to Andy Warhol, and such paintings as Jan Van Eyck's *Saint Jerome in His Study*, Pieter Bruegel the Elder's *The Wedding Dance*, and Rembrandt's *The Visitation*. It's also strong in German Expressionism.

NEARBY: The Heidelberg Project (600 Heidelberg Street) is Tyree Guyton's 30-year-old public-art experiment. In the McDougall-Hunt neighborhood of Detroit, which was damaged by riots in 1967, he began painting polka dots on the dilapidated houses. He added junk art and constructions of all kinds and expanded up and down the block. It has since become a model for art projects and social activism in forgotten urban environments.

DIEGO RIVERA, *DETROIT INDUSTRY*, 1933, DETROIT INSTITUTE OF ARTS, DETROIT, MI.
PHOTO: DWIGHT CENDROWSKI/ALAMY STOCK PHOTO

Milwaukee Art Museum

700 N. ART MUSEUM DRIVE
MILWAUKEE, WI 53202

Santiago Calatrava's addition to the Milwaukee Art Museum, a place that already had a butch-looking Eero Saarinen building and a Brutalist standout from David Kahler, brought the crowds it was intended to bring. Half engineer, half poet, Calatrava put "wings" on the Quadracci Pavilion that open at noon each day, turning the building into a colossal, kinetic sculpture in its own right. (Ultrasonic sensors automatically close them if winds top 23 m.p.h. so the building doesn't lift off.)

The museum, which dates back to the 1870s in one form or another, recently revamped the 2 older buildings, improving the galleries (many of which have epic views of Lake Michigan) and adding space for more collections to stay on view. It's strong on Fauvism and German Expressionist works, with standout paintings by Gabriele Münter and Paula Modersohn-Becker. It's also got one of Francisco de Zurbarán's most famous paintings, *Saint Francis of Assisi in His Tomb*, and one of the largest collections of Wisconsin-born painter Georgia O'Keeffe's work, including *Poppies*, *The Cliff Chimneys*, and *Lake George, Autumn*.

The new galleries have made more room for the museum's extensive Haitian art collection, including fantastical paintings by Rigaud Benoit. The contemporary sculpture galleries include one of Eva Hesse's last works, the 18-foot-long hanging piece *Right After*. On the lower levels, there's a new photo and video section with work by Ray Krueger Metzker, Diane Arbus, Garry Winogrand, and Robert Frank. There's also a trippy treat in Stanley Landsman's *Walk-in Infinity Chamber* made in 1968. (It's great to see this old classic hold its own against the proliferation of Yayoi Kusama's *Infinity Mirror Rooms* as museum-selfie bait).

NEARBY: In Burns Common on the east side of town is an impressive piece in Cor-Ten steel by Beverly Pepper. The 18-foot-tall *Cleopatra's Wedge* is pure power. Outside of town, in the suburb of Fox Point on Lake Michigan, is where artist Mary Nohl filled her yard with concrete sculptures of fish and people and monsters. It looks like Outsider yard art but it isn't—Nohl studied at the Art Institute of Chicago. After her death in 2001, the Kohler Foundation took over the site and narrowly avoided having to move it to appease the wealthy neighbors. There's now an art fellowship in her name as well.

You can't go inside but there's plenty to see from the street.

ALEXANDER CALDER, *RED, BLACK, BLUE*, 1973 (COMMISSIONED 1968), PAINTED METAL, MOTORIZED MOBILE, 40 FT. MILWAUKEE ART MUSEUM, LENT BY MILWAUKEE COUNTY GENERAL MITCHELL INTERNATIONAL AIRPORT, GIFT OF JANE BRADLEY PETTIT, 1987, L8. 2001.

PHOTO: MIKE REBHOLZ © CALDER FOUNDATION, NEW YORK / ARTISTS RIGHTS SOCIETY (ARS), NEW YORK

51

Walker Art Center

725 VINELAND PLACE
MINNEAPOLIS, MN 55403

MINNEAPOLIS INSTITUTE OF ART
2400 3RD AVENUE SOUTH
MINNEAPOLIS, MN 55404

Two great stops. The Walker is known for its ambitious exhibitions and for being an early champion of artists like Kara Walker, Robert Irwin, Barry McGee, and Catherine Opie. But its collection also includes paintings like Franz Marc's *The Large Blue Horses* and major pieces by Chuck Close, Yves Klein, and Edward Hopper. Its film department collects moving-image work from artists such as Matthew Barney, Nam June Paik, Stan Brakhage, Fernand Léger, William Klein, and Derek Jarman— all wrapped up in a spaceship designed by Herzog & de Meuron.

Its forward-looking nature includes multimedia arts, and it's been a pioneer of working on the web in conjunction with the other must-visit in town, Minneapolis Institute of Art. This McKim, Mead & White temple is a classic American city encyclopedia, collecting everything you could want to see to understand the culture of the world going back 5,000 years. Its highlights include several Louis Cranach the Elder portraits; Vincent van Gogh's *Olive Trees*; Do-ho Suh's large metal robe, *Some/One*; and Jennifer Steinkamp's digital projection into a rotunda. Outside is the bronze *The Fighter of the Spirit* by Ernst Barlach, a piece the Nazis tried to destroy in Kiel, Germany, but was hidden before they could get to it.

NEARBY: In front of the U.S. District Courthouse is one of Tom Otterness's phantasmagoric landscapes, called *Rockman*. Made up of a towering golem and multiple playful figures, it's an allegory about the power of the state that kids can crawl on.

CLAES OLDENBURG AND COOSJE VAN BRUGGEN, *SPOONBRIDGE AND CHERRY*, 1988.
PHOTO: GENE PITTMAN FOR WALKER ART CENTER, MINNEAPOLIS

52

The Art Institute of Chicago

111 S. MICHIGAN AVENUE
CHICAGO, IL 60603

The Art Institute of Chicago is home to some of the most famous paintings on earth: George Seurat's *A Sunday on La Grande Jatte*, Pablo Picasso's *The Old Guitarist*, Edward Hopper's *Nighthawks*, and Grant Wood's *American Gothic*. If that's all it had, you'd be happy you came. But the museum, right in the heart of the city's Loop, has enough to keep you busy for several days. Though it originated in 1866, its main building came with the 1893 Colombian Exposition, and after that the collection grew and grew and got a major expansion by Renzo Piano in 2009. The collections reach in every direction, with highlights including 30 paintings by Claude Monet, Vincent van Gogh's *The Bedroom*, Gustave Caillebotte's *Paris Street; Rainy Day*, Constantin Brancusi's *Golden Bird*, and major works by Eva Hesse and Joan Mitchell. A large portion of Alfred Stieglitz's archive is in the photography department, donated to the museum by Georgia O'Keeffe herself.

With all this blue-chip, top-of-the-line, irrefutably major stuff, one of the most likable things about the Art Institute is that it makes room for the shaggy and weird. It has the biggest collection of the American painter Ivan Albright, known as a magic realist, whose off-putting paintings have not been outdone by anyone deliberately seeking to creep since he did them in the 1940s. (He was even tapped to paint Dorian Gray for the Hollywood movie *The Picture of Dorian Gray*.) The institute also has the best collection of the Chicago Imagists—the postwar artists who took pop-culture inspiration from the comics (rather than advertising imagery, as the Pop artists in New York did). This includes H. C. Westermann's tattoo-like drawings and the great group the Hairy Who, which included Jim Nutt, Gladys Nilsson, and Karl Wirsum.

INSTALLATION VIEW OF THE EUROPEAN PAINTING AND SCULPTURE GALLERY WITH (CENTER) GEORGES SEURAT, *A SUNDAY ON LA GRANDE JATTE—1884*, 1884–86, OIL ON CANVAS, 81¾ x 121¼ IN. HELEN BIRCH BARTLETT MEMORIAL COLLECTION, 1926.224. THE ART INSTITUTE OF CHICAGO, CHICAGO, IL.

BACKGROUND LEFT: AUGUSTE RENOIR, *TWO SISTERS (ON THE TERRACE)*, 1881, OIL ON CANVAS, 39½ x 31⅞ IN. MR. AND MRS. LEWIS LARNED COBURN MEMORIAL COLLECTION, 1933.455. THE ART INSTITUTE OF CHICAGO, CHICAGO, IL.

BACKGROUND RIGHT: AUGUSTE RENOIR, *WOMAN AT THE PIANO*, 1875–76, OIL ON CANVAS, 36⁹⁄₁₆ x 29⅛ IN. MR. AND MRS. MARTIN A. RYERSON COLLECTION, 1937.1025. THE ART INSTITUTE OF CHICAGO, CHICAGO, IL.

PHOTO: THE ART INSTITUTE OF CHICAGO / ART RESOURCE, NY

53

Anish Kapoor's *Cloud Gate*

MILLENNIUM PARK
CHICAGO, IL 60601

Anish Kapoor's polished steel abstraction reflects Chicago's distinctive rows of office towers, the clouds and sky above it, and, most importantly, the faces and cameras of the millions of viewers who come to see it. "The Bean," as it's affectionately called, is engrossing in part because it never looks the same way twice, depending on the weather, the position of the viewer walking around it, and the global mix of fellow viewers twisting in the turns. In the right light, it appears weightless—it practically disappears. That Kapoor was inspired by liquid mercury is easy to grasp.

Made from 168 stainless-steel plates welded together and sanded to a seamless sheen, the 66-foot-long sculpture weighs an even hundred tons. Underneath the 12-foot-high "gate" that viewers can pass through is a surprise feature: the *omphalos*, or navel, that rises 24 feet into the structure and creates a multipart warped view of whatever is under it.

Cloud Gate went up in 2006 at a time when Chicago needed a shot in the arm, and it got it. The sculpture is the city's most visited attraction, and a globally recognized symbol. The trick is that it's more than one thing at once: It's both heavy and light; it's monumental and easygoing; and it looks luxurious but is also good, populist, Instagram-inducing fun. It's by a guy from India with an exotic name who also happens to have been knighted by the Queen of England.

NEARBY: Bridges by Renzo Piano and Frank Gehry lead away from the Bean. Piano's goes to his beautiful new wing of the Art Institute of Chicago (see p. 134), and Gehry's, an awkward swirl of titanium, leads out of the park, away from his self-plagiarized Pritzker Pavilion. The other major piece of art here is by Spanish artist Jaume Plensa, and, like the Bean, it also manages to be at once worldly and local, solid and ever-changing. Plensa put LED screens over the surfaces of two 50-foot towers with a reflecting pool between them, and runs clips of Chicagoans faces on them. The fun is that water spews from their mouths into the pools, turning them into high-tech gargoyles.

ANISH KAPOOR, *CLOUD GATE*, 2006, MILLENNIUM PARK, CHICAGO, IL.
PHOTO: RIO CHAVEZ

The Chicago Picasso

DALEY PLAZA
50 WEST WASHINGTON STREET
CHICAGO, IL 60602

Controversial when it was dedicated in 1967, this untitled 5-story Cor-Ten steel portrait of some kind of creature by Pablo Picasso has become a beloved icon of the city. It could be, in part, that the people love to gripe about it. To protest it while it was in development, a science-fiction writer erected a giant pickle on the site. Later, Chicago journalist Mike Royko said, "Its eyes are like the eyes of every slum owner who made a buck off the small and the weak. And of every building inspector who took a wad from a slum owner."

Picasso agreed to do it because, he said, he was also working on a piece for the city of Marseille, and this meant he'd be doing work for the world's 2 great gangster cities. He refused the $100,000 fee, making it a gift. The sculpture might not be among Picasso's most important pieces—the city is awash in Picassos, with the Art Institute holding *Man with a Pipe*, *The Old Guitarist*, and *Mother and Child*—but it was the first major piece of public art in this very conservative city that would go on to embrace adventurous and distinctive public art. (It also may be the tallest Picasso, though a town in Sweden claims its concrete bust of Jacqueline is the tallest.)

NEARBY: Across the street stands Joan Miró's 40-foot-tall figure *Chicago*, and a few blocks away, at 100 W. Randolph Street, there's a Jean Dubuffet called *Monument with Standing Beast* that viewers can walk through. The newest addition to the tradition of public art in the city is a 50-foot-long mural by Kerry James Marshall on the Cultural Center; it celebrates African American women, including Gwendolyn Brooks, Sandra Cisneros, and Oprah Winfrey.

THE CHICAGO PICASSO, 1967, DALEY PLAZA, CHICAGO, IL.

PHOTO: CAROL M. HIGHSMITH ARCHIVE, LIBRARY OF CONGRESS, PRINTS AND PHOTOGRAPHS DIVISION

Newfields

4000 MICHIGAN ROAD
INDIANAPOLIS, IN 46208

Newfields, an arts complex, includes the world famous Indianapolis Museum of Art and Oldfields, a 19th-century mansion with its own elaborate park whose name served as inspiration for the new, extensive project. The museum is one the great city temples of culture founded in the late 19th century, though this one doesn't have a Beaux-Arts building to hold it. Instead it lives on 152 acres and was designated to be an "acropolis" by the city in the 1960s, in a grand Edward Larrabee Barnes construction opened in 1970.

It's one of those museums that has everything up and down history and around the world, ranging from *A Thousand Peaks and Myriad Ravines*, the 1610 Ming dynasty painting by Wu Bin, to the *Magbo helmet mask* by master carver Onabanjo of Itu Meko. It's very strong on scrolls and screens from Japan's Edo period—which connects in spirit to its strong Post-Impressionism collection, including Emile Bernard's *Bretons in a Ferry Boat*; *The Channel of Gravelines, Petit Fort Philippe* by George Seurat; and Paul Gauguin's *The Flageolet Player on a Cliff*. It also has a large collection of work by J. M. W. Turner, a site-specific installation by Robert Irwin, and great American paintings like Edward Hopper's *Hotel Lobby*.

Oldfields is the mansion of the family of pharmaceutical industry giant

Eli Lilly, and in its complete restoration of architecture and decorative arts, has been called a Gesamtkunstwerk. The grounds also include the Miller House, moved here from Columbus, Indiana. It was designed by Eero Saarinen in 1957 and includes interior work by graphic designer Alexander Girard and landscaping by Dan Kiley. Last is the 100 Acres Art and Nature Park, which opened in 2010 with site-specific, often functional commissions by Alfredo Jaar, a basketball court by Cuban duo Los Carpinteros, a pair of giant rings that operate as a calendar by New York duo Type A, and a living space on an island by Andrea Zittel.

NEARBY: ArtsPark (820 East 67th Street) is a sculpture garden designed by Postmodernist architect Michael Graves to complement his Indianapolis Art Center building. The IAC is a community arts center and library that has put on shows such as one devoted to local boy George Rickey (they also help place his kinetic sculptures around town). In the park, you'll find pieces by Sadashi Inuzuka, Robert Stackhouse, Arnaldo Pomodoro, Truman Lowe, and John Spaulding.

EXTERIOR VIEW OF NEWFIELDS WITH ROY LICHTENSTEIN, *FIVE BRUSHSTROKES*, DESIGNED 1983–84 (FABRICATED 2012), PAINTED ALUMINUM, VARIOUS DIMENSIONS. INDIANAPOLIS MUSEUM OF ART AT NEWFIELDS, ROBERT L. AND MARJORIE J. MANN FUND, PARTIAL GIFT OF THE ROY LICHTENSTEIN FOUNDATION, 2013.443A-E.4 © ROY LICHTENSTEIN FOUNDATION

56

The Cleveland Museum of Art

11150 EAST BOULEVARD
CLEVELAND, OH 44106

A massive gem in the middle of Ohio, the Cleveland Museum started in 1913 as a Beaux-Arts Georgian temple and was later added to by Marcel Breuer in 1971 and Rafael Viñoly in 2009 and 2012. Most dramatic is a canopy of glass that spans a vast space between the wings, creating an area that's less gala-benefit atrium and more like a public square. The encyclopedic museum is known for its Egyptian and Asian art collections, but really spans the globe and millennia. Some standouts include Caravaggio's *The Crucifixion of St. Andrew*, J. M. W. Turner's *The Burning of the Houses of Lords and Commons*, Pablo Picasso's *La Vie*, George Bellows's *Stag at Sharkey's*, and Berthe Morisot's quieter but moving *Reading*. Postwar painters are well represented here, including Larry Poons, Morris Louis, Jules Olitski, Robert Mangold, and Mark Tansey. Out front is a notable early casting of Auguste Rodin's *The Thinker* that was blown up by the radical group the Weathermen in 1970 and stands, unrestored, bearing its scars like *Venus de Milo* or even *The Sphinx*.

NEARBY: Claes Oldenburg and Coosje van Bruggen created *Free Stamp* in 1992 as a commission for Standard Oil. The 50-foot-tall rubber stamp of the word "free" sits on its side in Willard Park, next to City Hall.

EXTERIOR AND GARDENS, CLEVELAND MUSEUM OF ART, CLEVELAND, OH.
PHOTO: © THE CLEVELAND MUSEUM OF ART

57

Toledo Museum of Art and the Glass Pavilion

2445 MONROE STREET
TOLEDO, OH 43620

The Toledo Museum of Art was founded by the glass titan Edward Libbey, who made Toledo into "the Glass City" and opened the museum in 1901. It was stocked from the beginning with his collections of glass art intended to inspire local workers, and that remains a core part of the collection today. It has items from ancient times to the Studio Glass movement of the 1950s, which was founded at the museum by Harvey Littleton and Dominick Labino.

The Toledo Museum of Art stands among the great city museums founded by industrialists with strong work from ancient Greece and Rome, the Renaissance, and Japan. Among its best paintings are Jean-Honoré Fragonard's *Blind Man's Bluff*, Thomas Cole's *The Architect's Dream*, and Vincent van Gogh's *House at Auvers*. Its Rubens—*Crowning of St. Catherine*—was once stolen by Nazi leader Hermann Göring and stored in a salt mine.

The museum expanded over the years, adding a Frank Gehry building in the 1990s and a wing, in 2006, that Nicolai Ouroussoff of the *New York Times* called an "elegant curving maze of glass," which recalls the Hall of Mirrors at Versailles. The Glass Pavilion was built by the Japanese firm SANAA and

provides a perfect space to show off the museum's see-through stuff.

LEFT TO RIGHT: WAYNE HUSTED FOR BLENKO GLASS COMPANY, DESIGN # 5929L IN PERSIAN BLUE (IN THE ARCHITECTURAL SERIES), 1959, MOLD-BLOWN, CUT AND POLISHED GLASS, 36 IN. TOLEDO MUSEUM OF ART, PURCHASED WITH FUNDS FROM HELEN BROOKS IN MEMORY OF MAYME AND RUDOLPH LUEDTKE, 2013.5A-B.

JOEL PHILIP MYERS, BLENKO GLASS COMPANY, DESIGN # 6535 L IN TANGERINE (PART OF ARCHITECTURAL SERIES), 1965, MOLD-BLOWN, CUT, AND POLISHED GLASS, 41½ IN. HIGH; DIAMETER: 10¾ IN. TOLEDO MUSEUM OF ART, PURCHASED WITH FUNDS FROM HELEN BROOKS IN MEMORY OF MAYME AND RUDOLPH LUEDTKE, 2013.6A-B

WAYNE HUSTED FOR BLENKO GLASS COMPANY, DESIGN # 5815-L IN LILAC (IN THE ARCHITECTURAL SERIES), 1958, MOLD-BLOWN, CUT, AND POLISHED, 36¼ IN. HIGH; DIAMETER: 11¼ IN. TOLEDO MUSEUM OF ART, GIFT OF DAMON CRAIN, 2013.166

WAYNE HUSTED FOR BLENKO GLASS COMPANY, SPOOL DECANTER WITH DIAMOND STOPPER, DESIGN #587-L IN JADE (IN THE ARCHITECTURAL SERIES), 1958, MOLD-BLOWN OF GREEN ENCASED IN TEAL GLASS, CUT, AND POLISHED, 35¾ IN. HIGH; DIAMETER: 6½ IN. TOLEDO MUSEUM OF ART, PURCHASED WITH FUNDS FROM HELEN BROOKS IN MEMORY OF MAYME AND RUDOLPH LUEDTKE, 2013.4A-B

WAYNE HUSTED FOR BLENKO GLASS COMPANY, DESIGN #5516WS (IN ARCHITECTURAL SERIES), 1955, MOLD-BLOWN, APPLIED, CUT AND POLISHED GLASS, 32¾ IN. HIGH; DIAMETER: 7½ IN. TOLEDO MUSEUM OF ART, PURCHASED WITH FUNDS FROM HELEN BROOKS IN MEMORY OF MAYME AND RUDOLPH LUEDTKE, 2013.3A-B

PHOTO: RICHARD GOODBODY INC.

58

Laumeier Sculpture Park

12580 ROTT ROAD
ST. LOUIS, MO 63127

GATEWAY ARCH
100 WASHINGTON AVENUE
ST. LOUIS, MO 63102

THE SAINT LOUIS ART MUSEUM
1 FINE ARTS DRIVE
ST. LOUIS, MO 63110

A soaring tribute to the West and the idea of progress and a better future, Finnish American Eero Saarinen's stainless-steel-clad structure is the tallest arch in the world, and America's biggest monument. Begun as an answer to a design competition in the 1940s (where he had to beat out his own dad, famous Cranbrook Academy of Art president Eliel Saarinen), it got taller by the time it opened in the 1960s, rising to 630 feet.

The idea seems almost brutish—a giant arch held up by reinforced concrete. But the final product is beautiful as the planes twist in and out of sight. It frames the St. Louis skyline and the clouds above it, and it rewards viewing up close much more than you'd think. The arch is about power—not all of it good (some of its history is stained by the removal of an African American neighborhood from the site)—and it's also a peak piece of modernism. There was a time when some of Saarinen's work was in danger of being written

off as future-kitsch, but these days, the Gateway Arch feels like a solid stop on the way from the Washington Monument to Anish Kapoor's *Cloud Gate* (p. 137).

More large forms are on view at the 72-acre Laumeier Sculpture Park. Here, the centerpiece is Alexander Liberman's 100 × 100 × 65 foot piece, *The Way*—as usual, made of discarded oil drums painted cadmium red, evoking a battleship's big guns and a cathedral all at once. It's his largest work, and definitely one of his best. Exuberant forms abound here—even the untitled Donald Judd sculpture feels far more provocative than his usual sober fare. Dan Graham created a playful triangular bridge and Beverly Pepper worked triangles, too, for her dramatic, traffic-cone orange piece *Alpha*. Cosimo Cavallaro and Robert Chambers both earn laughs with their pasta-like bronzes, and more overt humor comes from Niki de Saint Phalle's *Ricardo Cat* and Donald Baechler's *Flowers (Tulips)*. Readymades have fun, too: Alexandre Cunha put a found cement mixer on concrete blocks and Donald Lipski's *Ball? Ball! Wall! Wall!* is made up of 55 steel marine buoys stretching 300 feet through woods that other parks might have felt obligated to put an Andy Goldsworthy piece in. In fact, part of why the Laumeier is so refreshing is the absence of so many of the usual suspects, like Richard Serra, Claes Oldenburg, and the ubiquitous Roy Lichtenstein paint squiggles that seem to be on the rise. (Okay, the Laumeier did feel obligated to add a handful of Mark di Suvero's—but wouldn't you?)

Though they sprung for a Goldsworthy piece, the Saint Louis Art Museum offers up unexpected highlights such as local boy George Caleb Bingham's Luminist scenes from frontier life and an entire 350-foot-long cyclorama, *Panorama of the Monumental Grandeur of the Mississippi Valley* by John J. Egan, which depicts the region before the arrival of Europeans. It's now viewed as a scroll, instead of in the round. Small stars include Artemisia Gentileschi's *Danae*, painted on copper, and Marsden Hartley's *Driftwood on the Bagaduce*.

The museum was intended to be one of the great encyclopedic city museums springing up in the 19th century, and it excels at African art, Native American art, and textiles. It has made a point of collecting African American artists, including everyone from Henry Ossawa Tanner to Kara Walker. The photos by Moneta Sleet Jr., are a treat.

The Saint Louis Art Museum also holds the world's largest collection of Max Beckmann paintings, including his *Portrait of Curt Glaser* and the masterpiece *Christ and the Woman Taken in Adultery* from 1917. It was in the Nazis' Degenerate Art Exhibition of 1937, as was another more whimsical painting here, Matisse's *Bathers with a Turtle*.

DAN GRAHAM, *TRIANGULAR BRIDGE OVER WATER*, 1990, REFLECTIVE LAMINATED GLASS, ANODIZED ALUMINUM, PAINTED STEEL, AND CONCRETE, 84 × 192 × 120 IN. LAUMEIER SCULPTURE PARK COMMISSION, WITH FUNDS FROM THE NATIONAL ENDOWMENT FOR THE ARTS.
PHOTO: KEVIN J. MIYAZAKI

59

Nelson-Atkins Museum of Art

4525 OAK STREET
KANSAS CITY, MO 64111

It might seem like just another Neo-classical temple to the arts—in fact the architects Wight and Wight modeled it after the Cincinnati Museum. But out back, a series of glass pavilions feed light down to underground galleries creating caves that glow inside (by day) and out (by night). The addition by Steven Holl in 2007 was a refreshing change from the emphasis on soaring atriums in recently built museums across the country that lacked intimacy and made them less inviting for visitors.

The collection itself certainly didn't need any gilding. It's got Caravaggio's *St. John the Baptist in the Wilderness*, one of only 25 Hieronymus Bosch paintings in the world. The collection includes great German Expressionist work by Max Beckmann, Emile Nolde, Ernst Ludwig Kirchner and Oskar Kokoschka. Strong Asian sections include a pair of lifesize Yixian glazed pottery luohans (a disciple of Buddha), and one of only 8 from the Ming Dynasty discovered in a cave in the 1910s—they're said to be among the most important ceramic works in the world.

The museum has a collection of mostly American photography (given by Hallmark Cards chairman Donald Hall, Sr.) and an especially large collection of Native American art, including the extraordinary beaded work of Jamie Okuma who is part contemporary artist, part fashion designer. And there's a 5,000 square foot indoor garden of Isamu Noguchi's sculptures and fountains. Some more highlights include *Himmel*, by Marsden Hartley, from his insignia obsessed German series and John Singer Sargent's *Mrs. Cecil Wade*.

The Nelson-Atkins is especially strong on regional American painters; in fact it has the largest array of work by local hero Thomas Hart Benton, including his masterpiece *Persephone*.

NEARBY: Thomas Hart Benton Home and Studio (3616 Belleview). It never gets old peeping the palette knives and paint cans full of turpentine left behind in an artist's studio. You can do that here in the carriage house where Benton painted, next to his massive stone house.

THE BLOCH BUILDING OF THE NELSON-ATKINS MUSEUM OF ART, KANSAS CITY, MO.

PHOTO: MARK MCDONALD, COURTESY NELSON-ATKINS MEDIA SERVICES

South Central

The Philbrook Museum of Art

2727 SOUTH ROCKFORD ROAD
TULSA, OK 74114

With Kehinde Wiley's massive *Equestrian Portrait of Philip IV* installed in 2018 in the Italian Room of its 1920s oilman's mansion, Tulsa's Philbrook Museum shows its devotion to honoring both the past and all the forward motion of contemporary times. The painting is modeled after Velasquez's portrait, but like most of Wiley's work, it features an African American man, in exquisite street style, in the heroic role.

Waite Phillips surprised Tulsa just 10 years after moving in by turning the ornate Renaissance Revival villa, designed by Kansas City architect Edward Buehler Delk, and its 25-acre gardens, over to the city to create a museum. Later additions created more exhibition space and the Philbrook Downtown, a building in the Brady Arts District devoted to modern and contemporary art, and the institution's pride: its Native American painting collection. Spanning from ledger-style drawings of the Battle of Little Big Horn to Pop- and Expressionist-inflected American Indian Movement canvases, it's one of the best in the world. Much of the collection was generated by an annual show the Philbrook ran starting in 1946 devoted to Native American painting; some painters here include Narisco Abeyta, Woody Crumbo, Fritz Scholder, and

Oscar Howe. The Philbrook also presents a standout survey of Native American art in other mediums from basketry to jewelry to rugs to pottery masterpieces by Maria Martinez. Fittingly the main villa is stocked with Italian Renaissance art including work by Giovanni Bellini, but the museum also shows its breadth by including everything from work by 19th-century painter William Merritt Chase to contemporary sculptor Rachel Whiteread.

INSTALLATION VIEW OF **(CENTER)** BIAGIO D'ANTONIO, *THE ADORATION OF THE CHILD WITH SAINTS AND DONORS*, C. 1476, OIL ON LINDEN WOOD PANEL, 90½ x 86¼ IN. PHILBROOK MUSEUM OF ART, TULSA, OKLAHOMA. GIFT OF THE SAMUEL H. KRESS FOUNDATION 1961.9.19.

PHOTO: COURTESY PHILBROOK MUSEUM OF ART

Crystal Bridges Museum of American Art

600 MUSEUM WAY
BENTONVILLE, AK 72712

Straddling two rushing creeks, this museum devoted to American artists was created by Alice Walton and opened in 2011. The art world was dubious—what was the Walmart heir up to? But she used her considerable riches to create a top collection—including everyone from Charles Willson Peale to Thomas Eakins to John Singer Sargent to Edward Hopper to Mark Rothko—and a reputation for smart negotiations. The Moshe Safdie building of wood and glass displays the goods handsomely.

Some sleeper treats in the collection that shouldn't be missed include *War News from Mexico* by Richard Caton Woodville, *The Lantern Bearers* by Maxfield Parrish, and *Supine Woman* by Wayne Thiebaud. One of Kerry James Marshall's greatest paintings, *Our Town*, is here, as is an entire Frank Lloyd Wright house, the Bachman-Wilson House, shipped in from New Jersey. The museum ticks 3 of the sculptural/site-specific boxes every institution seems to have these days: a Roxy Paine, a Mark di Suvero, and a James Turrell Skyspace. But who can blame them for needing a Louise Bourgeois *Spider*?

NEARBY: If you come through Little Rock to get here, be sure to leave some time for the Arkansas Art Center (501 East 9th Street, Little Rock)—an institution with a devotion to works on paper that has earned it a major collection of Neo-Impressionist Paul Signac drawings and watercolors, an impressive array of Arthur Dove paintings and watercolors, drawings by Will Barnet, and a set of Robert Andrew Parker watercolors based on British poet Keith Douglas's World War II work.

VIEW FROM THE NORTH TO THE GALLERY BRIDGE WITH MARK DI SUVERO, *LOWELL'S OCEAN*, 2005–08, CRYSTAL BRIDGES MUSEUM OF AMERICAN ART, BENTONVILLE, AK.

PHOTO: DERO SANFORD, COURTESY CRYSTAL BRIDGES MUSEUM OF AMERICAN ART, BENTONVILLE, AK

Joe Minter's African Village in America

931 NASSAU AVENUE SW
BIRMINGHAM, AL, 35211

There's a tradition of artists setting up shop in their yards in the South and building and adding and expanding until every inch of them is filled. Call it self-taught, or Outsider, but true aficionados just call it art. Many of them have died or moved to the city—James Hampton and Lonnie Holley are some of the most famous ones around Alabama. But Joe Minter is still going strong, using his metalworking skills from his years as a construction worker to create his own world.

Born in 1942, Minter started to write out his thoughts about spirituality and the African American experience in the late 1970s. In 1988, though, he received a vision from God that led him to begin the African Village in America—totems inspired by African masks, signs, and paintings, all with an invented iconography related to black life and history. Plenty of it is very local and very real to Minter; his work commemorates the 16th Street Baptist Church bombing in 1963, and Martin Luther King Jr.'s stay in the Birmingham City Jail.

He draws from his own family's experience, too. His father fought in France in World War I and became a skilled mechanic. But back in the States,

racism, Jim Crow laws, and segregation made it impossible to earn a living using his trade, so instead he worked for 30 years in a cemetery. Minter became a skilled member of the U.S. Army, as well, in the 1960s, and also found himself getting by on odd jobs.

Minter's work is part of the Souls Grown Deep Foundation, started by William Arnett to study and preserve the rich and symbolic world African American artists created after the Civil War, as the agrarian economy of the South collapsed and people crowded near the new industrial centers for work. (The foundation organized the famous *The Quilts of Gee's Bend* museum show that toured the world for many years.) Through Souls Grown Deep's gifts to major institutions, Minter's work has gone into the collections of the High Museum of Art in Atlanta, the de Young Museum in San Francisco, and the New Orleans Museum of Art.

When Minter had his vision, the reclaiming of scrap was built in. "The whole idea handed down to me by God is to use that which has been discarded, just we as a people have been discarded made invisible," he told Arnett. "That what is invisible, thrown away, could be made into something so it demonstrates that even what gets thrown away, with a spirit in it, can survive and grow."

Minter has always been happy to talk to anyone who shows up. But now that he's older, he's not always available. If you're planning a visit, you can call the people who help manage the grounds at (205) 327-7370 to be sure

you get to meet the last major practitioner still outdoors.

Ogden Museum of Southern Art

925 CAMP STREET
NEW ORLEANS, LA 70130

There's something thrilling about a museum that can do many things that all hang together well; when it happens, it's because there's a vision guiding everything. The Ogden was put on this earth to celebrate art of the southern states—and it does it better than any other, with all of its disparate activities making sense together. It even has a historic building by an architect so associated with Boston it's a surprise to many that New Orleans is his hometown. H. H. Richardson— known for Trinity Church and Server Hall at Harvard University, as well as for his influence on Louis Sullivan— built a series of Romanesque Revival libraries in the late 1880s all over the country, but this is the only one in the South. It became part of the Ogden when it was founded in 1999. The interior space is spectacular, cathedral-like, and though it has some sculptures on display, it's mainly used for the Ogden's many public events involving southern music and literature.

The collection itself goes deep on artists like Walter Anderson, the vastly underrated painter of nature from nearby Ocean Springs, Mississippi, who battled schizophrenia, and Benny Andrews of Plainview, Georgia, who was well-trained at the Art Institute of Chicago but let a mixture of Southern folk art and Minimalism influence his mature work. There's Ida Kohlmeyer, the Louisiana native who studied with Hans Hofmann; George E. Ohr, the mad potter of Biloxi; and, of course, local hero Clementine Hunter (see more of her work near Baton Rouge, p. 161).

INSTALLATION VIEW OF SELECTED WORKS BY SIMON GUNNING, OGDEN MUSEUM OF SOUTHERN ART, NEW ORLEANS, LA.
PHOTO: SPENCER GREGORY

64

Clementine Hunter Home at Melrose Plantation

3533 HIGHWAY 119
MELROSE, LA 71452

Half an hour from Baton Rouge is a plantation that, by the late 19th century, had become a mixed-use situation: If you picked cotton by day, you could stay on and make art at night—it was an art colony. Clementine Hunter was the daughter of slaves and grew up picking cotton. She took a stab at painting almost by accident on an old window shade, and soon she was painting on bottles and jars and even on canvas. She lived to see her work celebrated—she once visited Jimmy Carter in the White House—and was collected by the likes of Oprah Winfrey and the Dallas Museum of Art. Robert Wilson even wrote an opera about her.

The plantation has 16 pieces in the front room of its "Big House," including some favorite motifs such as Hunter's obsessive love of zinnias and a giant chicken pulling a cart, but the real prize is in the round "African House" out back, where there are 9 painted panels depicting all of life in the Cane River Valley where Hunter grew up. There are pictures of sharecroppers at work, kids playing in the river, baptisms, and a wedding.

Hunter's work falls into the category of Outsider Art or folk art, and its excitement—its joy—comes from the way she worked from memory, and without care for devices like perspective. Hunter said, "Painting's a lot harder than picking cotton. The cotton is right there for you to pick it, but to paint, you've got to sweat your mind."

NEARBY: There are several other spots to see great examples of Hunter's work in the area, including at the Natchitoches Parish Library (450 2nd Street, Natchitoches), and the LSU Rural Life Museum and Gilley's Gallery in Baton Rouge. But the best way to absorb more of Hunter's ethos may be to simply drive around the Cane River and see the landscapes she knew as a girl and captured in her paintings.

INTERIOR VIEW, MELROSE PLANTATION, AFRICAN HOUSE, MELROSE, LA.

PHOTO: LIBRARY OF CONGRESS, PRINTS & PHOTOGRAPHS DIVISION, HABS LA,35-MELRO, 1B--32 (CT)

Kimbell Art Museum

3333 CAMP BOWIE BOULEVARD
FORT WORTH, TX 76107

**AMON CARTER MUSEUM OF
AMERICAN ART**
3501 CAMP BOWIE BOULEVARD
FORT WORTH, TX 76107

**MODERN ART MUSEUM OF
FORT WORTH**
3200 DARNELL STREET
FORT WORTH, TX 76107

If you're going to show the only Michelangelo painting in the Western Hemisphere, you'd better not mess up the lighting. Architect Louis Kahn captured a silvery glow that still astounds visitors to the building that houses the Kimbell, erected in 1966. Made up of 16 barrel-vaulted galleries inspired by ancient Rome, the structure is widely regarded as one of the best, if not the single best, museum buildings of the second half of the 20th century.

The beneficiary of the perfectly proportioned spaces is a collection that includes Caravaggio's *The Cardsharps*, Annibale Carracci's *The Butcher's Shop*, and Gustave Caillebotte's *Le Pont de l'Europe*. There are portraits by El Greco, Tintoretto, Diego Velázquez, and Théodore Géricault, and work from other cultures as well, including Africa and Asia. There is one American artist's work in the entire collection: Isamu Noguchi's *Constellation (for Louis Kahn)*.

Just a block up Camp Bowie Boulevard is a museum that started off with a narrow specialty but then grew beyond its niche. Starting with newspaper publisher and philanthropist Amon Carter's collection of 250 Frederic Remington paintings, the Amon Carter Museum of American Art opened in 1961 to showcase art about the Old West—the romanticized version of cowboys and broncos and (not always fairly represented) Native Americans. The museum, designed and expanded by architect Philip Johnson over the decades, has the world's top collections of Remington and the other master of this genre, Charles Russell. It has every bronze by either, and hundreds of their paintings and drawings. *A Dash for the Timber*, also in the collection, launched Remington's career when the Connecticut-based painter showed it in New York. It's his finest painting, and it helped shape views of the Old West that carried on into Hollywood Westerns.

The Amon Carter's mission expanded to include all kinds of visions of the West—and has paintings of the frontier from George Catlin, John Mix Stanley, and Albert Bierstadt, as well as works by John James Audubon. It showed what was only the third ever retrospective of Georgia O'Keeffe's work in 1966, and she attended. (The museum has several major paintings of hers, including *Ranchos Church, New Mexico* and *Red Cannas*.) Dorothea Lange also showed up for the opening of her own show, which went on to tour the world. A Lange print was the first photo at the Amon Carter, and it sparked a large and important collection that includes the complete work of Laura Gilpin, who documented the Hopi and Navajo nations extensively.

In 1967, the museum acquired Stuart Davis's late work *Blips and Ifs*—and announced it was not hung up on covering the West anymore, but would broaden its view to collect all American art. That new focus brought in many more by Davis, including *Bass Rocks No. 2*, as well as other early American modernists such as Marsden Hartley, Charles Sheeler, Charles Demuth, and Arthur Dove (represented by one of his greatest works, *The Lobster*).

On the other side of the Kimbell is the imposing Modern Art Museum of Fort Worth—a series of 5 pavilions by Tadao Ando that seem to float on a 1.5-acre pond. The galleries are stunning spaces, with 40-foot-tall windows and stark granite floors. Highlights of the collection include paintings by Morris Louis, Philip Guston, and Mark Bradford; photography by Catherine Opie, Cindy Sherman, and Andres Serrano; and Martin Puryear's *Ladder for Booker T. Washington*.

NEARBY: A few blocks away at Foch and 7th Street stands a rooftop Martin Creed neon-sign sculpture—this one says *Mothers*. Best seen at night, of course.

EXTERIOR VIEW OF THE KIMBELL ART MUSEUM, DESIGNED BY LOUIS KAHN, WITH HENRY MOORE, *FIGURE IN A SHELTER*, 1983, FORT WORTH, TX.

PHOTO: ROBERT LAPRELLE. © 2013 KIMBELL ART MUSEUM, FORT WORTH

Dallas Museum of Art

1717 NORTH HARWOOD STREET
DALLAS, TX 75201

It's huge—and like all the big city museums, spans many millennia and cultures. Its roots were in the Dallas Art Association, which showed Texan painters in the public library starting in 1903, and it went through several homes before it got its vast Edward Larrabee Barnes building in 1984.

Some of those early painters who showed in the library made up the Dallas Nine, devoted to painting the Southwest, including Otis Dozier, William Lester, and Everett Spruce. They were realists, not romantics like the Western painters, and they brought some Impressionist technique along for the ride. The Dallas Museum of Art has the biggest collection devoted their work (there were a lot more than 9 of them).

But the rest of the galleries feature plenty of work by big American and European painters; some standouts are Frederic Edwin Church's *The Icebergs* from 1861; Gerald Murphy's *Razor*, and his biggest painting, *Watch*, from 1924; Robert Rauschenberg's *Skyway*, which references JFK's assassination in Dallas; and a small collection of paintings by Piet Mondrian. Postwar work includes strong paintings by all the New York School heavies, the Germans—Gerhard Richter, Sigmar Polke, and Anselm Kiefer—and photography by Cindy Sherman, Lynn Davis, and Charlie White.

The Impressionists and Post-Impressionists are represented in the main collection, but also take center stage in a 15,000-square-foot re-creation of Coco Chanel's villa La Pausa in the South of France. Given by Emery Reves, who bought it in the 1950s, it includes a collection of small works by Paul Cézanne, Edgar Degas, Paul Gauguin, Édouard Manet, Claude Monet, and Vincent van Gogh, as well as dozens of Pissarros and Renoirs.

The museum takes the decorative arts seriously, and has a large collection of modern design, including the front doors to a Greene & Greene house in Pasadena and work from Ettore Sottsass and the Campana Brothers. A recent acquisition is a knockout: the Wittgenstein Vitrine by Carl Otto Czeschka—a 5-foot-tall silver case encrusted with gems, made in 1908.

The worth-the-trip-alone moment here is right outside the front door: a 60-foot-long glass mosaic by Miguel Covarrubias, made in 1954 for an office building overlooking the city's first major freeway. Covarrubias was born in Mexico City but made a name for himself in Manhattan in the 1920s

doing caricatures for *Vanity Fair* and the *New Yorker*. Back in Mexico, he became interested in preserving and analyzing pre-Columbian art, which influenced his mature work, like this masterpiece devoted to the 4 elements.

NEARBY: At the Dallas County Records Building (1201 Elm Street), artist Lauren Woods has built a piece into a drinking fountain, originally labeled "Whites Only," from the Jim Crow era. Woods removed a plaque that covered the remnants of that sign and added a video projection of Civil Rights protesters being attacked by police with firehoses. The video is triggered when a visitor drinks. It's one of several pieces around town that Woods has

made, outside of the normal art-world venues, to highlight past oppression of African Americans in Dallas.

OPPOSITE: INSTALLATION VIEW OF THE EUROPEAN GALLERIES AND (ABOVE) THE EXTERIOR VIEW, DALLAS MUSEUM OF ART, DALLAS, TX.

Nasher Sculpture Center

2001 FLORA STREET
DALLAS, TX 75201

There are not many museums where sculpture is the boss. There are plenty of parks and plazas, roofs and rotundas where 3-dimensional art rules, but once you've got walls, most places think flat. Raymond and Patsy Nasher started their collection with pre-Columbian artifacts, but they wound up breaking the 7-figure barrier 20 years later when they bought *Large Seated Nude* by Henri Matisse. The collection grew to include great examples of sculpture's modern all-stars: David Smith, Barbara Hepworth, Henry Moore, Constantin Brâncuși, Alberto Giacometti, Alexander Calder, and a 100-foot-long Richard Serra. The collection became so famous, everyone wanted it—the Tate, the Guggenheim, and more—but the real-estate developer and mall king and his wife got Renzo Piano to build a little masterpiece for it in their hometown of Dallas.

The building is cool and elegant. It's filled with natural light, thanks to Piano's system of egg-like skylights, and the very gently arched ceilings give it buoyancy (and an echo of Louis Kahn's building for the Kimbell Art Museum in Fort Worth [p. 163], which Piano would later design an addition for). Also, the Nasher's interior goes easy on the walls: Three long pavilions divided by travertine slabs run the length of the building which is entirely glass at the front and back. You can see straight through it from the street to the garden, and it's perfect for sculpture and the kinds of thoughtful shows the Nasher curators put on, which always factor in the space between objects.

The one-and-a-half acre garden has its Mark di Suvero, its Tony Cragg, and James Turrell's *Tending (Blue)*, a black box with a Skyspace-like hole in the top that some say was ruined by the Museum Tower next door. Like the Kimbell's, the collection is tightly edited—there are only some 300 objects in it—but there are always some gems to be rotated into view, like the messy little bronze nudes of Willem de Kooning, the colorful fun of Joan Miró, the powerful ceramic work of Peter Voulkos, and the late-career balancing acts of Joel Shapiro. (The Nasher does collect some flat art—almost exclusively preparatory works by sculptors.)

It's not all textbook greats. The Nasher puts on temporary shows that push the boundaries of the medium and explore very current messages (and it loans its collection to the Dallas/Fort Worth airport). The Nasher Prize was started in 2015, going to Doris Salcedo, and since has been awarded to Pierre Huyghe and Theaster Gates.

The Nasher is flanked by the Dallas Museum of Art and that problematic Museum Tower—which caused a little more trouble when the reflections off its windows were so intense they were burning up the trees in the sculpture park below.

INSTALLATION VIEW WITH: TONY SMITH, *FOR DOLORES*, CA.1973–75, CARRARA MARBLE, 44¼ x 44¾ x 45¼ IN. RAYMOND AND PATSY NASHER COLLECTION, NASHER SCULPTURE CENTER, DALLAS, TX. ALBERTO GIACOMETTI, *SPOON WOMAN (FEMME CUILLÈRE)*, 1926 (CAST 1954), BRONZE, 56¾ x 20 x 9 IN. RAYMOND AND PATSY NASHER COLLECTION, NASHER SCULPTURE CENTER, DALLAS, TX. AUGUSTE RODIN, *THE AGE OF BRONZE (L'AGE D'AIRAIN)*, CA. 1876, PLASTER, 71½ x 25½ x 21¼ IN. RAYMOND AND PATSY NASHER COLLECTION, NASHER SCULPTURE CENTER, DALLAS, TX.

PHOTO: CAROLYN BROWN

The Menil Collection and Rothko Chapel

1533 SUL ROSS STREET
HOUSTON, TX 77006

1409 SUL ROSS STREET
HOUSTON, TX 77006

A block apart, but both created by the oil heiress Dominique de Menil and her husband, John, the 30-acre Menil Collection and the Rothko Chapel campus share a desire to let art speak for itself. The main building houses the collection, with its focus on surrealism, modern European painting, and post-war American art. Two other buildings house single-artist collections, one of work by Cy Twombly, which includes *Untitled (Say Goodbye Catullus, to the Shores of Asia Minor)*, and one of work that Dominique commissioned from Dan Flavin.

The Menil Collection opened in 1987 in a building by Renzo Piano. The collection's early 20th-century works include those by René Magritte, Max Ernst, Yves Tanguy, Marcel Duchamp, Henri Matisse, and Pablo Picasso. There's all the New York School and Pop Art crew, and a smattering of Byzantine, African, Tibetan, and Pacific Northwest art. Some surprisingly great pieces include drawings by Charles Houghton Howard, Jasper Johns's *Bushbaby,* and a Robert Smithson drawing from 1961, *Blind Angel.*

The Cy Twombly Gallery building was opened in 1995 and spans the artist's entire career. Given his connections to ancient art, philosophy, Abstract Expressionism, and Pop Art, it's a pretty good mirror for the Menil tastes. And the delicacy of his lines—many pencil on canvas—benefit greatly from Piano's mastery of natural light for museums.

Mark Rothko received his commission in 1964 and created 14 paintings for a nondenominational chapel now considered to be one of the most emotionally moving pieces of art in the country. It didn't open until 1971, months after Rothko took his life following years of depression. The Rothko galleries have been the setting for meetings by world leaders, including the Dalai Lama, Desmond Tutu, and Nelson Mandela, and also inspired a major modernist piece of music by Morton Feldman.

There's a Barnett Newman *Broken Obelisk* (another stands in the atrium at MoMA) that the Menils gave the city of Houston in honor of Martin Luther King Jr. The city declined, so it's here, atop a reflecting pool designed by Philip Johnson.

RIGHT: INSTALLATION VIEW OF SELECTED WORKS BY JOAN MIRÓ, FERNAND LÉGER, AND ALEXANDER CALDER, MENIL COLLECTION, HOUSTON, TX.
PHOTO: DON GLENZER.

PAGES 170–71: THE ROTHKO CHAPEL, HOUSTON, TX.
PHOTO: RUNAWAY PRODUCTIONS

69

Ellsworth Kelly's *Austin* and Blanton Museum of Art

THE UNIVERSITY OF TEXAS AT AUSTIN

200 EAST MARTIN LUTHER KING JR.
BOULEVARD
AUSTIN, TX 78712

Ellsworth Kelly's been called the "Happy Modernist" and it shows in this just opened chapel space at the University of Texas's Blanton Museum. White with geometric cutouts filled with colored glass, it's a space that feels pure and hopeful without being trite. Two hundred miles away, the Rothko Chapel (p. 168), however moving and transcendent, suddenly seems like a big downer. *Austin* was Kelly's last work, and it's a hell of a way to go out. Inspired by Byzantine architecture, the structure is like 2 intersecting barns with colored windows at each end—each with a different geometric pattern. The *New York Times* called it "the grandest exploration of pure color and form in a seven-decade career spent testing the boundaries of both," and also compared it to major works by Christo, Michael Heizer's *City*, the Chinati Foundation in Marfa, Henri Matisse's *Chapelle du Rosaire de Vence*, and Le Corbusier's *Notre Dame du Haut*.

The Blanton, at 180,000 square feet, is the country's biggest university museum, and its collection includes ancient art and Renaissance paintings. It has a 20th-century American painting collection given by the writer James Michener that includes Thomas Hart Benton, Alice Neel, and Brice Marden. Contemporary artists added to the collection include El Anatsui, Nina Katchadourian, and Charles White. Its Latin American collection is strong, too, including Diego Rivera, Rufino Tamayo, and Wifredo Lam.

Also on the UT campus is Landmarks, a treasure hunt of a public art collection, with Louise Bourgeois, Ann Hamilton, Marc Quinn, Michael Ray Charles, Magdalena Abakanowicz, and Nancy Rubins.

NEARBY: The *Hi, How Are You* mural (at 21st and Guadalupe) is emblematic of everything Austin loves about itself: It's weird. Painted by Outsider artist Daniel Johnston—a musician whose music has been covered by Tom Waits and Beck, and whose art has made it into the Whitney Biennial—it's simply a frog saying, "Hi!"

ELLSWORTH KELLY, *AUSTIN* (INTERIOR, FACING SOUTH), 2015, ARTIST-DESIGNED BUILDING WITH INSTALLATION OF COLORED GLASS WINDOWS, BLACK AND WHITE MARBLE PANELS, AND REDWOOD TOTEM, 60 FT. x 73 FT. x 26 FT. 4 IN. BLANTON MUSEUM OF ART, THE UNIVERSITY OF TEXAS AT AUSTIN, GIFT OF THE ARTIST, WITH FUNDING GENEROUSLY PROVIDED BY JEANNE AND MICHAEL KLEIN, JUDY AND CHARLES TATE, THE SCURLOCK FOUNDATION, SUZANNE DEAL BOOTH AND DAVID G. BOOTH, THE LONGHORN NETWORK, AND OTHER DONORS. © ELLSWORTH KELLY FOUNDATION

PHOTO: COURTESY BLANTON MUSEUM OF ART, THE UNIVERSITY OF TEXAS AT AUSTIN

#70

Chinati Foundation

1 CAVALRY ROW
MARFA, TX 79843

Marfa, a small town in West Texas, is Mecca for the art world. It was a normal town, with an old army base that held German prisoners of war during World War II. But in 1971, Donald Judd left New York City for Marfa, bought a couple of ranches, and with the help of the Dia Art Foundation, acquired Fort Russell in 1979. He envisioned spaces that would hold large single-artist collections, and, after his death in 1994, the Chinati Foundation and the Judd Foundation continued that mission over the 340-acre property. There are buildings devoted to Dan Flavin, Ingólfur Arnarson, Roni Horn, John Chamberlain, Ilya Kabakov, Carl Andre, and David Rabinowitch.

The cavalry's former horse stable is the only significant space devoted entirely to underrated Pop artist John Wesley's paintings, including a batch he did at Marfa inspired by Chinati's collections. The cavalry also inspired a 20-foot-high horseshoe by Claes Oldenburg and Coosje van Bruggen dedicated to the last horse who lived there, named Louie. It also has the only freestanding structure built as a Robert Irwin art piece—an indoor/outdoor meditation on light and space that rivals any art-chapel experience, including Rothko's in Houston.

The star of the show, of course, is Judd. There are 2 massive vaulted military sheds devoted to 100 untitled pieces in mill aluminum—made for the spaces in the 1980s. All of them are the same dimensions—41 × 51 × 72 inches—but their interiors are all variations. Judd didn't just plop them in the spaces, though—he altered the entire building, its windows, ceiling, and floor, so that it really is one big art piece, not 100 separate ones. He took the same approach at the Arena, a building he altered so much that even its functional spaces are part of the art. His 15 massive untitled pieces in concrete seem to hold the whole place down to earth at the edge of the property.

There's something about the spare landscape of a desert coupled with the mostly Minimalist work inside the vast hangers that combines to deliver a truly powerful experience. It's a place to take your time, stay a few days. Also at Chinati is a gallery and artist-residency program run by the International Women's Foundation in the old Officers Club with its curious Western-landscape murals painted by a couple of German POWs.

There's much more Judd in store when you visit his private residences and studios in several buildings around town. The studios let you see his furniture in real living spaces along with early work such as drawings and paintings. Visits are by tour and appointment only, and worth planning way ahead for.

In town there's also the Ayn Foundation, which shows Andy Warhol's *The Last Supper* and Maria Zerres's "September Eleven" series.

Chinati's status as an art destination picked up speed in the 1990s as the foundations expanded and other art organizations opened, such as Ballroom Marfa. In fact, an entire dusty, Minimalist, vaguely Native American–adjacent aesthetic began to take over the town and creep out into mainstream culture. Vintage hotels were retrofitted to appeal to visitors from the coasts, and some of the art energy in town began veering toward "artsy."

Poking fun at all this hit its peak when the artists Elmgreen & Dragset opened what looked like a Prada store out on Highway 90. Standing starkly, ridiculously, in the desert, the door doesn't work but the glass display windows hold real merchandise from the luxury brand. The "sculptural intervention" itself pokes fun at commercialization of art, at Prada's own pared-down aesthetic, at the attempt to escape the consumer-focused art world that Marfa represents, at Land Art, at all kinds of things. What seemed to some like a one-liner at first has held onto its ability to create different meanings for visitors (and survived at least one major attempt to vandalize it).

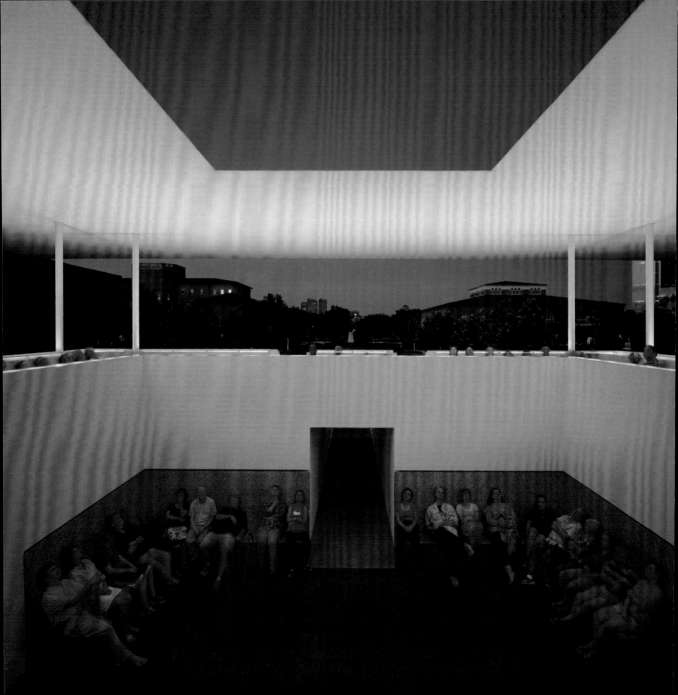

James Turrell's *Twilight Epiphany* Skyspace

SUZANNE DEAL BOOTH CENTENNIAL
PAVILION, RICE UNIVERSITY
HOUSTON, TX 77005

MUSEUM OF FINE ARTS, HOUSTON
1001 BISSONNET STREET
HOUSTON, TX 77005

There are many James Turrell Skyspaces across the country now, and the experiences of colored light against the changing sky in their open roofs are always meditative and absorbing (at least where cell phone use is strictly not allowed). But when one stands out, and manages to surprise you, it's worth a trip. At Rice University, Turrell placed the room inside a mound on a campus quad, with a rectangle that seems to hover above its open roof. Where most Skyspaces are hidden from the outside, this one creates sci-fi effects for viewers inside and out since the hovering rectangle and the shifting colors projected on it are visible around the campus. The sunset viewings are sought after, and a reservation is recommended. The less-popular sunrise viewings are perfection.

About a 5 minute drive away, is the Museum of Fine Arts, Houston. With buildings by Mies van der Rohe, Rafael Moneo, Morphosis, and Steven Holl (and a sculpture garden designed by Isamu Noguchi), it's hard to imagine that the museum's collection is not upstaged by its buildings. There's something of an obsession with gold here, with separate impressive collections devoted to gold objects from Africa, Indonesia, and the pre-Columbian Americas. The museum also exhibits strong Impressionist, Post-Impressionist, and Fauvist work.

The painting sections have greats by Frederic Edwin Church, George Bellows, Childe Hassam, Mary Cassatt, and the entire roster of Paris moderns and New York School kids seem to be here—but the museum also digs deeper into corners of American art history, exploring Synchronism, the first abstract art in the United States, with key works by Patrick Henry Bruce, Stanton Macdonald-Wright, and Morgan Russell. The collection looks at the Taos Society of Artists and the Alfred Stieglitz group with Marsden Hartley, John Marin, Helen Torr, and Georgia O'Keeffe (see *Grey Lines with Black, Blue and Yellow*). One lovely highlight is André Derain's *The Turning Road, L'Estaque*.

One of the really distinctive areas that MFA Houston mines is concrete and constructivist work from South America, including work by the Brazilians Lygia Clark, Waldemar Cordeiro, and Hélio Oiticica, as well as a mother lode of kinetic sculpture. There are also spaces devoted to early 20th-century Latin American masters such as Diego Rivera, David Alfaro Siqueiros, Joaquín Torres-García, Armando Reverón, Wifredo Lam, Rufino Tamayo, and Roberto Matta; and they take an aggressive stance on contemporary work from the region including art by María Fernanda Cardoso, Los Carpinteros, Alfredo Jaar, Guillermo Kuitca, Teresa Margolles, Cildo Meireles, and Gabriel de la Mora.

JAMES TURRELL, *TWILIGHT EPIPHANY*, 2012, SUZANNE DEAL BOOTH CENTENNIAL PAVILION, RICE UNIVERSITY, HOUSTON, TX.

PHOTO: FLORIAN HOLZHERR.

Ant Farm's *Cadillac Ranch Show*

13651 I-40 FRONTAGE ROAD
AMARILLO, TX 79124

ROBERT SMITHSON'S *AMARILLO RAMP*
TECOVAS LAKE
AMARILLO, TX

A subversive idea that has become a free-floating pop-culture icon, this row of junked Cadillacs planted nose down (and at the same angle as the walls of the Pyramids of Giza) traces the history of the extravagant tailfins on a car that carries so much meaning in America. It was created by Chip Lord and Dave Michaels, a team who went by the name of Ant Farm. They wanted to be more like a rock group than an art collective, and got their name from a girlfriend's reaction to them calling what they did "underground architecture."

Lord, Michaels, and later Hudson Marquez, planned *Cadillac Ranch Show* from the heart of the counterculture revolution in San Francisco and, needing sponsorship, cold-called Amarillo Oil heir Stanley Marsh III almost at random from a list of millionaires. The eccentric Marsh bit, and went on to commission other sculptures and art projects on his vast ranches, including Robert Smithson's last work, *Amarillo Ramp.* Both were completed in 1974.

Cadillac Ranch was moved to a site more accessible to the highway in 1997, and somewhere along the line the gutted cars—which range from vintage 1949 to 1963—became a blank canvas for graffiti and other repaintings. Visitors pull off the road—once Route 66 of the song and kitschy motel signage—and cross a fence to paint and take selfies and run amok. It's an exuberant scene.

Ant Farm took as its main subjects consumerism—the Cadillac's absurdly elongated and pointless tailfins being the perfect symbol of success and excess in midcentury America—and media; its most famous piece is *Media*

Burn, a performance at the Cow Palace outside of San Francisco in which a Cadillac was crashed full speed into a pyramid of operating TV sets.

What *Cadillac Ranch* means now is wonderfully muddled, itself having become a kind of nostalgic roadside attraction from a bygone era of family road trips.

Also on formerly Marsh-owned land is Robert Smithson's *Amarillo Ramp*, his last major work, due to the fact that he was killed in a plane crash while surveying the site. The piece was finished after his death by his wife, the Land Art artist Nancy Holt—who built *Sun Tunnels* in Utah (p. 193)—as well as Richard Serra and the gallerist Tony Shafrazi. The ramp was conceived as

the last in a trilogy of spirals—*Spiral Jetty*, in the Great Salt Lake (p. 190), being the first, and *The Broken Circle*, in Holland, being the second. It was built of red shale in a lake bed, with the slope rising and turning over 163 feet from the middle of the water. Like much of Smithson's work, it's about entropy, and was meant to eventually dissolve back into the earth.

Like *Spiral Jetty*, *Amarillo Ramp* dissolved much faster than expected, and Holt led efforts to maintain the piece until her death in 2014. Volunteer art students from West Texas A&M make the trip twice a year to the now-dry lake bed and fight back mesquite and cholla cactus and do what they can to shore up the *Ramp*.

It's very difficult to visit *Amarillo Ramp*: Visitors must arrange through the operators of the cattle ranch in Amarillo (Coyote Bluff Cattle Company) to be taken by jeep to the site, and weather can scuttle the trip at any time. If you do make the drive, it's recommended to listen to Lee Ranaldo's record, *Amarillo Ramp*, a tribute to the artwork and Smithson by the Sonic Youth guitarist, which builds quietly and slowly, like the ramp, over 30 minutes.

Mountain

Tippet Rise Art Center

96 SOUTH GROVE CREEK ROAD
FISHTAIL, MT 59028

There might not be a more spectacular setting for sculpture in America: 11,500 acres of working ranchland in pristine Montana. With nothing but snow-capped peaks behind a massive piece of art, anything would look good—and Alexander Calder's *Two Discs,* on loan from the National Gallery of Art, certainly does. If you think you're tired of Mark di Suvero (even though he can do no wrong), look at his 6-story-tall *Proverb* with the Beartooth Mountains behind it.

The proprietors are Cathy Halstead, the painter daughter of the late booze billionaire Sidney Frank, and her pianist husband, David, who opened the ranch to the public in 2016. Given their interests, the cultural efforts are split between music and art—with structures having been built for the music with top acoustical engineers. One is a barn made from local timber in the vernacular style, the other is a sculptural shell on posts that can provide shade for an audience of 100, and amplify performers' music.

The taste in sculpture is not too different. Stephen Talasnik produced a series of structures made of tangled rods meant to face the elements on their own terms. (A bamboo commission spread over 3 acres of Storm King Art Center, p. 45, survived an earthquake, a hurricane, and record snowfall.) Another architectural art piece is a replica 19th-century schoolhouse, overcome by a cloud of twigs made by Patrick Dougherty.

But the payoff for the long drive here is the truly thrilling and new work of Antón García-Abril and Débora Mesa's Ensamble Studio from Madrid—strange, organic structures that look like they've been here for millennia (and they have, since they're made entirely from material excavated at the ranch). *Beartooth Portal*—a pair of bivalve-like shells propped up against each other to make a mystical gate—looks both like a natural occurrence and a project from an earlier civilization (perhaps assisted by aliens). *Domo* is a pair of inverted-cone-shaped mountains—upside down volcanos—even more otherworldly. The duo have been known for experimental architecture projects all over the world, but these are solid art hits.

Tippet Rise is only open to the public a few days a week in the summer, and reservations are imperative. The art pieces can be as far as 3 miles apart from each other, so expect to spend 2-and-a-half hours in the tour van, or half a day if you hike or mountain bike. Occasional music events in the off-season might provide a peek at the sculptures.

NEARBY: The Yellowstone Art Museum (401 North 27th Street, Billings) is absolutely more interesting than you might expect—the buffalo dioramas, as great as they are, are down the road at the Natural History Museum. Here you'll find the Montana collection—art about the West from artists including Freeman Butts, Deborah Butterfield, Jaune Quick-to-See Smith, and Peter Voulkos.

A collection of Abstract Expressionists gives the back bench of the movement a chance to shine, with work by the likes of Jack Tworkov, Emerson Woelffer, Felix Ruvolo, Herman Cherry, and Robert DeNiro Sr. And being Montana's recipient of the Vogel 50X50 donation (in which civil-servant collectors Dorothy and Herbert Vogel bequeathed 50 works each to single museums in 50 states with the help of the National Gallery), there are drawings by people like Will Barnet and Richard Tuttle here.

And a jewel of this collection—a discovery for most—are some 800 works by Isabelle Johnson, a former student of the Skowhegan School in Maine who made a home in Montana and brought modernist ideas about art to her work painting the landscape, and to students she taught for 50 years.

ENSAMBLE STUDIO, *INVERTED PORTAL*, 2015. TIPPET RISE ART CENTER, FISHTAIL, MT.

PHOTO: ANDRE CONSTANTINI

Denver Art Museum

100 WEST 14TH AVENUE PARKWAY
DENVER, CO 80204

You might not expect the biggest museum between Chicago and Los Angeles—one with its origins dating back to 1893—to go in for high drama. But that's what the Denver Art Museum did in 1971 when it opened its twin-towered castle by Italian-design genius Gio Ponti. In 2006, it did it again with a deconstructivist explosion of an expansion by Daniel Libeskind. Meant to evoke the jagged angles of the Rocky Mountains, its otherworldly presence is almost violent upon approaching. Inside, the flights of stairs through its 4-story atrium—bisected with slivers of light and with surprising twists and turns—are thrilling (though the space has been criticized as terrible for actually showing art).

The museum had always been bold; one of its decisions in the 1920s led it to be one of the strongest collections of Native American art in the world. The museum was among the first institutions to approach native work from a purely aesthetic point of view—it was art, not ethnography. Now nearly every tribe in North America is represented with particular strength in ceramics and 19th-century Arapaho beadwork. It's also strong on contemporary Native American artists such as Fritz Scholder. The approach has led to great galleries in African and Oceanic work

as well. (And the museum has excellent collections of Asian, Spanish colonial, and pre-Columbian art).

The painting collection does well in Impressionism and Post-Impressionism, and has some older pieces by Thomas Gainsborough, Hans Holbein the Younger, and Benjamin West. In its modernist and postwar rooms, there are works by Georgia O'Keeffe, Marcel Duchamp, and all the postwar movements you'd expect, including a large collection of work by Robert Motherwell. Design geeks will enjoy the complete archives of Bauhaus polymath Herbert Bayer.

The museum has been the beneficiary of many gifts of Western art—enough to establish the Petrie Institute of Western American Art. It has major works by Charles Russell and Frederic Remington, as well as pieces depicting the West by Thomas Moran, Albert Bierstadt, and the Taos Society's Ernest L. Blumenschein. The museum also houses Red Grooms's *Shootout*—controversial because of its dated cowboys vs. Indians premise. It's housed by the restaurant, as if to keep it at arm's length.

NEARBY: Just reopened in mid-2018, the Kirkland Museum of Fine and Decorative Art (1201 Bannock Street) is the vision of Colorado modernist painter Vance Kirkland, and it shows its art and objects all mixed up, salon style, inspiring multiple reference points. A room might mix furniture by Alvar Aalto or Gio Ponti or Frank Lloyd Wright with sculptures by the likes of George Rickey and

Robert Mangold, and paintings by unsung Colorado modernists like Watson Bidwell, Ken Goehring, Dave Yust, and Kirkland himself.

INTERIOR VIEW OF THE DANIEL LIBESKIND BUILDING OF THE DENVER ART MUSEUM, DENVER, CO.

Clyfford Still Museum

1250 BANNOCK STREET
DENVER, CO 80204

Concrete slabs, thin, variegated, and arranged vertically, make up the facade of the museum dedicated to the work of Abstract Expressionist Clyfford Still. The rough surfaces connect with Still's palette-knife techniques, and the strips echo the orientation of his compositions, without mimicking them. Still was part of the New York School, and lived and worked in Maryland from 1951—after he'd turned his back on the commercial art world—until his death in 1980. But his painting always seems of the West. He was born in Nebraska and came of age in tough times, painting workers in brutal circumstances. In the 1930s, he co-founded the Nespelem Art Colony in Washington State to preserve and advance native art there, and made his breakthroughs to abstraction while teaching at the California School of Fine Arts (the forerunner of the San Francisco Art Institute), and hanging out with Mark Rothko.

He showed in New York at Peggy Guggenheim's Art of This Century gallery and later with Betty Parsons, and is credited with creating Abstract Expressionism ahead of his better known contemporaries, especially Jackson Pollock. His shapes, while entirely nonobjective, can evoke the primordial drama of Western landscapes, and are often said to speak to man's struggle with nature—even if critic Robert Hughes teased them for their "Night-on-Bald-Mountain jaggedness of silhouette" in his book *The Shock of the New* (referencing Modest Mussorgsky's symphony, which had been turned into pop culture by the Disney movie, *Fantasia*).

The museum made art-world news because it was the answer to a decades-old riddle about Still: Why was the prime mover of Ab Ex a footnote after Barnett Newman and the rest? Where were all his paintings? After exiting the art biz, Still kept painting—and his will stipulated that the work he had, which amounts to 95 percent of his life's total output, go to one city that would build a perfect museum for it. In 2004, it was announced that Denver had stepped up to the plate and Still's widow, Patricia, had approved the museum, to be designed by Allied Architects. It opened in 2011 and, partly because it has the cream of the crop, not the leftovers, it's being called one of the most successful single-artist museums in the world.

It would be tempting to try to squeeze a visit to the Clyfford Still Museum on the same day as the massive Denver Art Museum (p. 186) next door. That's a mistake. The museum deserves thought and time, as does Still, whose place in art history is justified and restored here.

INSTALLATION VIEW OF SELECTED WORKS BY CLYFFORD STILL, INCLUDING *PH-247*, 1951, *PH-4*, 1952, AND *PH-238*, 1951, CLYFFORD STILL MUSEUM, DENVER, CO.

PHOTO: © RAUL GARCIA, COURTESY CLYFFORD STILL MUSEUM

Robert Smithson's *Spiral Jetty*

ROZEL POINT AT GREAT SALT LAKE
NEAR CORINNE, UT 84307

The goal of Land Art was to seek a bigger canvas—a bigger room—than the studios and galleries could provide. But when applied to *Spiral Jetty*, Robert Smithson's 6,000-ton array of boulders intruding into the Great Salt Lake, the term still seems too small. Smithson was inspired in part by the Nazca Lines—miles-long ancient stone drawings in Peru, which modern humans only made sense of once they had the power to fly over them. Smithson's subject wasn't scale, it was time—geological time; time on the biggest conceivable scale. He knew environmental conditions would eventually erode his creation—he even referred to the project as a "collaboration with entropy." It didn't matter to Smithson that it would be gone—he thought over decades the piece would be experienced slipping away, as "an erasure," and that objects were merely "the excrement of thought and language." He wanted *Spiral Jetty*'s eventual absence to be as important as its presence.

He got what he wished for much sooner than he expected. Built in 1970, it was completely submerged by 1972, and for the most part has only been known by aerial photographs and the film he directed, *Spiral Jetty*. Its sudden disappearing act has lent the work and the site a sense of mystery, of myth. The fact that it has "risen" periodically in its eroded form—such as in the mid-2010s, as a result of a local drought—only adds more to its legend. Smithson never saw it after 1972—he died in a small airplane crash in 1973 while surveying his final piece, *Amarillo Ramp*, in Texas (see p. 180).

Spiral Jetty is under the stewardship of the Dia Art Foundation, which provides updates on viewability on its website. The site is very remote, with no facilities whatsoever. At the time of publication, visitors could walk the full length of *Spiral Jetty*, which exists more as an outline of moist salt than the original boulders. Don't wear your best shoes. And go see it before it slips away again.

If you're feeling extra intrepid, a few hours away is *Sun Tunnels* (p. 193), created by Smithson's wife, Nancy Holt, in 1973. In the same way that *Spiral Jetty* takes on all of the earth's history, *Sun Tunnels* makes a canvas of the entire solar system, interacting as it does with the sun and stars. Both can be seen in one day of hard driving.

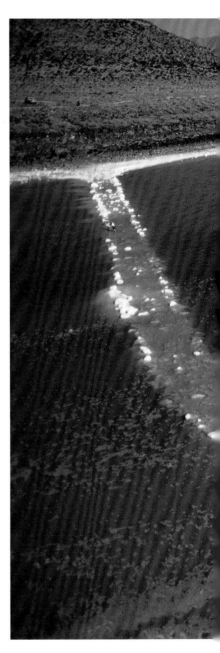

ROBERT SMITHSON, *SPIRAL JETTY*, 1970, GREAT SALT LAKE MUD, SALT CRYSTALS, ROCKS, WATER, 1500 FT. LONG x 15 FT. WIDE. COLLECTION OF DIA CENTER FOR THE ARTS, NEW YORK.

PHOTO: GEORGE STEINMETZ, COURTESY DIA ART FOUNDATION, NEW YORK. ART © HOLT-SMITHSON FOUNDATION/LICENSED BY VAGA, NEW YORK, NY

Nancy Holt's
Sun Tunnels

GREAT BASIN DESERT
NEAR LUCIN, UT 84083

One of Land Art's major works, *Sun Tunnels*, by Nancy Holt, appears simple—and minimal—when you approach the site outside the ghost town Lucin. Four concrete pipes, 9 feet tall and 18 feet long, form a skewed *X* on the flat, cracked clay ground. But Holt, who got her start in photography and film in the 1960s before going on to create art installations all over the world, has much more in store for the visitor. When the sun rises and sets on the days of the summer and winter solstice, it lines up perfectly in the tunnels—and this is how the work is most famously photographed. But at the beginning or end of any day, the tunnels frame the vistas and the light and each other like a giant camera, and the concrete picks up the surrounding color as it moves. These big, inert objects are rendered much more powerful and mysterious as a result.

Land Art was often described as utilizing "a bigger canvas," and many of the artists compared what they were doing to drawing on the earth. The site of *Sun Tunnels* is 83 feet across (on a 40-acre plot of land Holt bought in 1973), but with its reach to snow-capped mountains on all sides, it's truly hundreds of miles wide. In fact, by boring holes in each tunnel that shine light forming the constellations of Draco, Perseus, Columba, and Capricorn, she has brought astronomy into the piece—and was the first Land artist to do so.

"*Sun Tunnels* was a way of bringing the universe back to human scale," Holt said in several interviews. The artist was already immersed in New York's Post-Minimal downtown art scene—and close to Eva Hesse, Richard Serra, and the others—when she first visited Las Vegas with her husband, artist Robert Smithson, and Michael Heizer, and felt profoundly changed by the expanses of the West. Using tubes to reframe how people experienced the landscape and sky was already an idea brewing when she finally found the site. Holt died in 2014, and in 2018 the Dia Art Foundation acquired *Sun Tunnels* in a partial gift from the Holt-Smithson Foundation; *Sun Tunnels* is the first piece of Land Art by a woman in Dia's collection.

There are no services nearby, and 4-wheel drive is recommended. There are also no signs at all leading you to *Sun Tunnels*, which is the way Holt wanted it.

NANCY HOLT, *SUN TUNNELS*, 1976, GREAT BASIN DESERT, UTAH.

PHOTO: NANCY HOLT, COURTESY THE HOLT-SMITHSON FOUNDATION. ART © HOLT-SMITHSON FOUNDATION/LICENSED BY VAGA, NEW YORK, NY

Sego Canyon and the Great Gallery in Horseshoe Canyon

OFF INTERSTATE 70 IN
SOUTHEASTERN UTAH

When we think of cave paintings, we tend to be stuck on Lascaux in France and Altamira in Spain as the ne plus ultra. If we can't make it to see the best, why see or learn about any? But there are ancient wall drawings, some painted on pictographs, some pecked in petroglyphs, all over America, some left by the earliest descendants of Native Americans, some from people before them who remain mysterious. Cave buffs will debate any claim about which is best—the recently discovered drawings in Tennessee's Cumberland Gap may be the oldest, dating back to 5000 BC; the ones at the Wells Preserve in New Mexico might be the best preserved. But the southeast corner of Utah, right off Interstate 70, offers a primer on the 3 major kinds of petroglyphs in the U.S., and without having to hire a guide or rent a boat or a rock-climbing harness.

Sego Canyon has Barrier Canyon–style pictographs on one face dating back some 2,500 years. On another face are Fremont-style petroglyphs from about 1,200 years ago. A mere 500 or so years ago, the Ute people started adding pictographs. What's interesting is that these different artists obviously knew about each other's work—they didn't destroy the earlier drawings, or attempt to cover them up with their own. It's documentation of art history in action—influence passing down over thousands of years—and it's not in a vault or a Neoclassical temple. It's exactly as it was left.

The earliest drawings are from the Archaic period, going back up to 7,000 years, when nomadic people lived in the area. These are mostly pictographs with life-size humanoid figures. They usually have no arms or legs, but some do have antennae, large, insect-like eyes, or skull-shaped heads.

Twenty-one miles away, in Horse-shoe Canyon, there are about 80 of these life-size figures in the Great Gallery. One figure is 9 feet tall, with much more detail than the others—clearly the boss.

The Fremont people were part-time farmers in the area beginning around 600 A.D., and were neighbors of the more famous Anasazi culture. The petroglyph figures are geometric—triangular bodies and rectangular heads—but with adornments, like necklaces and headpieces, that we can recognize from later Native cultures.

The Ute drawings you can see at Sego Canyon are probably from the 19th century; they depict white men, horses, buffalo, and shields. They've been vandalized to some degree, but for the most part are very clear and crisp.

ELABORATE AND WELL-PRESERVED BARRIER CANYON STYLE PETROGLYPHS, SEGO CANYON, UT.

PHOTO: THOMAS FROM USA (FREMONT CULTURE ART UPLOADED BY PDTILLMAN)

79

Michael Heizer's *Double Negative* and *City*

SOUTHERN NEVADA

Michael Heizer is the last great Land Art madman alive. Smithson was its rock star who died in a plane crash. Nancy Holt produced works that incorporated time and the universe in surprising ways, and she died pretty young, too. Walter De Maria hung on long enough to be called one of the greatest artists of the 20th century but died with plenty left to do. Charles

Ross is plugging away at *Star Axis* in New Mexico, but it's reportedly pretty polished at this point.

Heizer created *Double Negative* in a period spanning 1969 and 1970, and displaced 240,000 tons of rock to do so. It's a quarter-mile-long trench that cuts through the landscape, Mormon Mesa, and has presence even in the spaces it crosses that are empty. It's strange, unsettling, and brings up questions of earth time vs. human time and the notion of creation by subtraction. It's not far from Las Vegas, but the route on unpaved roads and footpaths is tricky. (Heizer's website gives very good directions and advice.)

Meanwhile, Heizer's project *City* is completely cloaked in secrecy. He's

been working on it since 1972 on land he bought near Hiko, Nevada. If you find the address and head out there, you'll be met with a locked gate. *City* is a mile and a half long, and much of it is inspired by the Native American mound-building that Heizer learned about from his anthropologist father and while working on earlier works like *Effigy Tumuli* in Illinois (an update on ancient drawings meant to be seen from space). Some of the existing structures that have been photographed appear to be 8 stories high, and all materials used in construction are being mined at the site.

With support from the Dia Art Foundaton and LACMA (not to be confused with L.A.'s MOCA, which

owns *Double Negative*), the work is expected to be completed by the spring of 2020. Limited tours will be offered in spring and fall.

NEARBY: If you were to drive between the sites, you'd hit Las Vegas. It's not worth its own trip, but the deceptively named CityCenter (a mall with a collection of high-end hotels at 3780 South Las Vegas Boulevard) does have some big names in its art collection, including a classic, flat Frank Stella from 1969, a striking Maya Lin piece in silver based on the twists of the Colorado River, a 250-foot-long Jenny Holzer sign, a massive Nancy Rubins explosion of boats that you can only see from a tram, and work by Henry Moore, Tony Cragg, Donald Judd, Isa Genzken, and Julian Schnabel. Oh, and there's a James Turrell to enjoy while waiting for the elevator.

Southwest

Georgia O'Keeffe's Home and Studio

21120 US-84
ABIQUIÚ, NM 87510

Probably the most satisfying visit in this book. Not only is the house and studio that Georgia O'Keeffe built from a dilapidated hacienda intact, the landscape and its power over the imagination is unchanged. O'Keeffe began spending time in the area after visiting Mabel Dodge Luhan in Taos in 1929. Soon she made it a regular summer getaway from both New York and her husband, Alfred Stieglitz. She worked and painted in a secluded corner of Ghost Ranch, driving around in a Ford Model A to find the rock formations and ravines that would become her most famous landscapes. In 1945, she bought the land in the village of Abiquiú. When she built her new spot, she used traditional adobe building techniques but added modern skylights and picture windows to bring in light: The doorways and windows were the subjects of many of her paintings—as were the views of the cottonwood trees below in the Chama River Valley. She moved here full-time in 1949, 3 years after Stieglitz's death. Some people who visited her at Abiquiú include Charles Lindbergh, Allen Ginsberg, Joni Mitchell, Eliot Porter, and Ansel Adams.

The trivia and the game of spotting compositions fall away quickly here. Among artists' homes, the closest thing to it is Winslow Homer's house on the Maine coast (p. 13). The similarity is in that the surroundings that captivated the artists—the powerful work of nature continually paying humanity no mind—is practically overwhelming.

A few miles drive from O'Keeffe's home is the White Place, an area of dramatic rock formations and cliffs, all white, that she painted many times. Spot the Cerro Pedernal from here, a flattop mountain of which O'Keeffe said, "It's my private mountain. It belongs to me. God told me if I painted it enough, I could have it."

The Georgia O'Keeffe Museum in Santa Fe runs the tours of the house at Abiquiú—and you can see a good survey of her work there, from flowers to skyscrapers to bones, including *Black Hollyhock Blue Larkspur*, *Untitled (City Night)*, and that amazing blue void in *Pelvis IV*.

There are two kinds of tours at Ghost Ranch—one on foot that goes to her old home (nothing left compared to Abiquiú), and one that goes by van to locations she painted. Some of the most thrilling places to compare to her paintings aren't at either location. The Black Place, which inspired 14 years of work, is 150 miles east of Ghost Ranch—its desolate hills are immediately recognizable. O'Keeffe compared them to a field of 100 elephants.

THE ROOFLESS ROOM IN GEORGIA O'KEEFFE'S HOME, ABIQUIÚ, NM.

PHOTO: HERBERT LOTZ, GEORGIA O'KEEFFE MUSEUM, SANTA FE / ART RESOURCE, NY

Taos Pueblo and Art Colony

TAOS, NM

This town is brimming with artists and has been for something like a thousand years. The Taos Pueblo is the oldest continuously occupied pueblo culture site—dating back to at least 1000 A.D. Its 5-story main building went up sometime before the 1400s. Drawn by traditions still going strong here, American and European artists started coming at the start of the 20th century, and by 1915, the Taos Society of Artists was founded. Big personalities tumbled through town, including D. H. Lawrence, Georgia O'Keeffe, Agnes Martin, and Dennis Hopper, casting shadows in every direction.

There are nearly a dozen small, fascinating museums in this town, but the Millicent Rogers rates as one of the best for Native American arts anywhere. Its pottery collection from Pueblo people from all over the region includes masterworks by Maria Martinez—the woman from San Ildefonso Pueblo just south of here who revived Pueblo black-on-black pottery, or black ware, in the 1910s. Soon after, museums all over the world began to collect it. The collection also includes Navajo textiles, baskets from many regions, Hopi Kachina dolls, and Rogers's own extensive collection of Navajo silver-and-turquoise jewelry. The museum was very early to recognize the need to preserve Hispanic American art—which developed in distinctive ways here because of the difficulty of importing goods from Spain.

The founding Taos Society painters included Joseph Henry Sharp, who first came in 1893, Ernest L. Blumenschein, and Bert Geer Phillips. They began painting the local Native Americans in realist and Impressionist techniques, but without the romanticism many of the Western painters had used for decades. They soon branched out to the rest of the culture around the area, painting Hispanic laborers and hacienda life. By 1917, there were shows of their work touring the United States and their influence began to be felt. Three of their homes have become museums, all made up of small pueblo and Spanish-style houses stitched together over the years, and all interesting. The former home of Nicolai Fechin, who came to paint in 1923, has become the main museum for the Taos Society painters—with over 800 pieces from the group in its collection.

Another home worth a quick stop—though it's not a museum—is the Mabel Dodge Luhan House, just outside of town. Dodge Luhan was a perfect patron of the arts for the time: an heiress with a bob and a bohemian bent. Beginning in 1917, she set out to create a salon for the Taos art colony. She lured D. H. Lawrence and his wife, Frieda, to come work in Taos in the 1920s—the relationship was the source of plenty of drama. Many notables came to visit, including Georgia O'Keeffe, Frida Kahlo, Willa Cather, Aldous Huxley, Robinson Jeffers, Ansel Adams, and Edward Weston. It was bought by Dennis Hopper who moved to Taos to do the final edit on his film *Easy Rider* in 1969, and now it's a hotel with most of its original furniture and detail intact. (One oddity in town, the Hotel de la Fonda, makes much of its permanent show of D. H. Lawrence's forbidden paintings—a set of 9 softcore paintings that were confiscated in London after the *Lady Chatterley's Lover* brouhaha).

Art moved on, but artists kept coming to Taos. The Taos Moderns soon took the place of the society, and included Louis Ribak, Clay Spohn, and Beatrice Mandelman. The Harwood Museum, another group of buildings stitched together and now associated with the University of New Mexico, has the best collection of this work, including work by John Marin and Marsden Hartley done when they visited. Contemporary Native American artists are represented by the likes of R. C. Gorman and Tony Abeyta, and there's a more extensive look at local Hispanic pieces at the Harwood, including tin Santos icons. The museum also features the next wave of artists who gravitated here in the 1970s, like ceramic-sculpture pioneer Ken Price and Light and Space art kingpin Larry Bell, who followed Hopper out from Venice Beach.

Agnes Martin wound up nearby when she lost her rent-controlled loft in Manhattan's Coenties Slip and decided to check out on the world. She built her own adobe house, painted, and kept to herself until 1993 when she moved into Taos and stayed until her death in 2004. The Harwood Museum of Art has a gallery devoted to her—an 8-sided space with an oculus at the

top and 4 yellow benches made by her friend Donald Judd. It's a perfect room. Visitors can contemplate 8 of Martin's paintings that she donated to the museum for this purpose, with their relentless horizontal lines. As seen at Dia:Beacon and in SFMOMA's little Martin room, her work benefits from a little distance from the Sturm und Drang of the contemporaries she's often lumped with in collections. Martin herself was a frequent visitor to this gallery in her final years.

The sense that you're rubbing shoulders with artists of all kinds when you're walking around Taos is constant, and if you run into Larry Bell, who still spends half his time here, by all means say hello—he's about the most gregarious artist you'll ever meet (there's a very boisterous bar back in Venice Beach that's still named after him). He may invite you to his studio in what was once a large auto garage in town, and he's never stopped inventing in the Light and Space vein he helped pioneer in the 1960s.

INSTALLATION VIEW OF AGNES MARTIN GALLERY, HARWOOD MUSEUM OF ART, TAOS, NM.

PHOTO: COURTESY THE HARWOOD MUSEUM OF ART, TAOS, NM

82

Heard Museum

2301 N. CENTRAL AVENUE
PHOENIX, AZ 85004

Treating Native American culture as vital and alive is key to the Heard Museum's success. Founded in 1929 from Dwight and Maie Bartlett Heard's collection, it has grown into one of the most important museums in the Southwest. Its charming, Spanish-style main building doesn't show off the 50,000 square feet of expansions it's had through the years. It's also the biggest museum that makes it a point to see native art, old and new, from the first-person point of view rather than from an analytical or anthropological perspective. That means it has great relationships with artisans who've received knowledge from generations of makers, and also with contemporary artists collaborating with the museum.

The Heard's collections divide into 2 areas. One is a deep look at work made throughout the Southwest, including the best collection of Hopi Kachina dolls in the world, Navajo and Zuni jewelry, Navajo textiles, ceramics from prehistory to the present, and basketwork extending into California. The museum enlists contemporary Native American artists to guest curate these shows in order to preserve that first-person point of view—helping to upend placement of art objects in ethnographic contexts for decades.

The other main drive is contemporary art—especially from the Native American Fine Art movement started in the 1960s. As Native American artists began using Western art techniques in the early 20th century, and experimenting with modernist ideas in the postwar era, they were always bedeviled with challenges over tradition and authenticity.

Humor is key, according to painter Jaune Quick-To-See Smith. "Humor is a tie that binds tribe to tribe," she says. "Humor is a panacea for what ails"—and also contains

powerful social criticism. You can see humor at work in pieces like T. C. Cannon's 1980 painting of an Osage man in traditional dress sitting at home in front of a van Gogh wheatfield painting.

The Heard continues to collect contemporary work, and has re-created the studio of the New Mexican painter Pablita Velarde. She was one of the leading Native painters of the 20th century who worked in the "flat painting" style, did murals on pueblo life for the WPA, and showed all over the world. The museum also puts on the Native American Art Market Fair each March, which represents over 100 tribes and has been running for over 60 years.

NEARBY: There are two James Turrell Skyspaces nearby. Your basic round model is at the Scottsdale Museum of Contemporary Art (7374 East Second Street, Scottsdale). The more interesting is *Air Apparent*, at the Arizona State University Tempe campus (which is also, appropriately, home to the interdisciplinary School of Earth and Space Exploration). Based on local Hohokam tribe dwellings, the concrete and steel structure housing the piece feels light and ephemeral set in its Christy Ten Eyck cactus garden. No reservation needed; you can drop by 24/7.

OPPOSITE: INSTALLATION VIEW OF *BEAUTY SPEAKS FOR US*, HEARD MUSEUM, PHOENIX, AZ.

ABOVE: ENTRY COURTYARD, HEARD MUSEUM, PHOENIX, AZ.

PHOTOS: CRAIG SMITH

Pacific Coast
and
Hawaii

Seattle Art Museum

1300 FIRST AVENUE
SEATTLE, WA 98101

OLYMPIC SCULPTURE PARK
2901 WESTERN AVENUE
SEATTLE, WA 98121

The Seattle Art Museum is in a fun, complicated building made by the godfather of Postmodernism, Robert Venturi, who famously spoofed Mies van der Rohe by saying "Less is a bore." The museum's name is carved in giant letters outside, a nod to his influential book written with Denise Scott Brown, *Learning from Las Vegas*. There's a grand entry stair, presided over by giant Ming-era stone figures, that echoes those of the Metropolitan Museum of Art and the Louvre (pre-I. M. Pei). Exploring the collection is an adventure because of the layout of the galleries and Venturi's effort to switch up the experience for viewing different kinds of art.

The collection itself—the biggest and best in the region, strongest in non-Western art—has everything from the *Judgement of Paris* by Lucas Cranach the Elder to contemporary artist Saya Woolfalk's science fiction-like multimedia "virtual chimeric space," *Chimatek*. But one of its real prides is its collection of Pacific Northwest art—the carved masks and totem poles by the area's Native Americans.

Just a short 10 minute drive away is one of the very best sculpture placements of all time, Alexander Calder's *Eagle* at the Olympic Sculpture Park where you can watch over the ships hustling through Puget Sound. Richard Serra's *Wake*—10 Cor-Ten steel plates, each 14 feet high—also seems inextricable from its site, having been made using machines designed to cut ships' hulls with a wave-like shape to them. One major work that was created for the park is Teresita Fernández's *Seattle Cloud Cover*—a 200-foot glass bridge over railroad tracks with layers of color that alter the view of the city and sound and cast brilliant light on both the walkway and the visitors themselves. Aside from strong Beverly Peppers and Tony Smiths and a major Mark di Suvero, you can get the most pleasure sitting on Louise Bourgeois's *Eye Benches*—3 sets of surreal stone eyes with droopy lids that can hold your bottom.

Also noteworthy is that Seattle Art Museum runs the Asian Art Museum in Volunteer Park, though it's closed for renovations until mid-2019.

INSTALLATION VIEW OF *NATIVE ART AND LIFE ALONG THE NORTHWEST COAST* AT THE SEATTLE ART MUSEUM, SEATTLE, WA.

PHOTO: MARK WOODS.

Oliver Ranch

22205 RIVER ROAD
GEYSERVILLE, CA 95441

A lonely 8-story concrete tower is the center of the action at this former sheep ranch in California's wine country, now an expansive sculpture "park." It turns out to have been created by multimedia installation artist Ann Hamilton, and is one of her only permanent works. It has no roof, and the inside is entirely taken up by two spiral staircases forming a double helix. It's a performance space where the audience can face the performers on many levels.

It took almost 4 years to build, and that's fine with Nancy and Steve Oliver, a family who made their money in construction locally, and who see Oliver Ranch as a series of personal relationships with artists. Each of the 18 works of art on the land is site-specific, and each artist's direction was simply to respond to the landscape.

The first commission, in 1985, was by Judith Shea, and the colossal classically carved stone face turned on its side on a path is in keeping with her other mysterious games with art history. Later commissions demonstrate an astounding amount of patience and open-mindedness on the part of the benefactors—and prove their promise to not see any of the art as a commodity that can eventually be sold off.

Andy Goldsworthy, best known for stone walls and huge balls of twigs, made a set of installations that were temporary, with only a couple of them even being allowed to be documented. Bill Fontana created a sound piece— 5 speakers installed around a lake pumping in low-frequency noise from 5 points around the globe. Frustration is even embedded into the experience of some of the works: Martin Puryear built an elaborate stone gate that leads to a freestanding cave—but the entry is permanently blocked by a cedar lattice.

Oliver Ranch tends to bring out the architectural impulse in many of its artists (where many site-specific pieces for sculpture parks respond to their landscape by altering the earth itself, or framing views). It may be because part of the Olivers' program includes ready assistance from Steve and his heavy-duty construction equipment. Bruce Nauman built a 1,320-foot-long staircase that follows rolling hills across the land, the depth of the risers altering with the elevation, making walking them a deliberately awkward game. Miroslaw Balka, regarded as one of Poland's greatest living artists, poured a concrete footprint mirroring his childhood home (it's his only outdoor sculpture in the United States). Robert Stackhouse and Ursula von Rydingsvard also built elaborate structures, hundreds of feet long, that a visitor can weave in and out of. (Of course, every sculpture park worth its salt has to have a Richard Serra piece, and Oliver Ranch does.)

And then there's Hamilton's *The Tower*, which has hosted performances for 6 tubas by composer Tony Zilincik; a commissioned piece from composer Pauline Oliveros called *Tower Ring*; and pieces calibrated for the space by Kronos Quartet and Meredith Monk.

The performances at the tower all raise money for arts-related nonprofits, as do the walking tours of the ranch led by Steve. It's the only way to see the sculpture park—a group makes an appointment and a donation to a non-profit art group of their choice; then they get a 2-and-a-half-mile, 3-hour tour from Steve. (Individuals can contact Oliver Ranch and try to join a group's already scheduled tour.)

BRUCE NAUMAN, *UNTITLED*, 1998–99, AT OLIVER RANCH, GEYSERVILLE, CA.

PHOTO: ALEX FRADKIN

85

Fine Arts Museums of San Francisco

THE LEGION OF HONOR MUSEUM
LINCOLN PARK
100 34TH AVENUE
SAN FRANCISCO, CA 94121

THE DE YOUNG MUSEUM
50 HAGIWARA TEA GARDEN DRIVE
SAN FRANCISCO, CA 94118

The 2 old-school museums in San Francisco joined together as 1 unit in 1972, despite being the centerpieces of 2 separate city parks, miles apart. The Legion of Honor is that beloved museum of dreams for people who grew up here: The Neoclassical building among the windswept oaks overlooking the Golden Gate Bridge embraces you with an entry courtyard. The whole place is an elegant jewel, just right for an hour or 2 of seeing spectacular Old Masters and baroque treasures. There's a couple of El Grecos, Peter Paul Rubens's *The Tribute Money*, and the must-see *Bust of Cosimo* by Benvenuto Cellini. The museum's most famous painting is William-Adolphe Bouguereau's *The Broken Pitcher*, and a couple more not to miss include Jean-Léon Gérôme's Orientalist fantasy *The Bath*, and late Pre-Raphaelite John Roddam Spencer Stanhope's masterpiece *Love and the Maiden*.

The Francophile collection does well with everything Paris-related from the 1880s to the 1920s. The Achenbach Foundation for Graphic Arts (AFGA) is the largest collection of works on paper in the U.S., with drawings and prints by everyone from Rembrandt to Diebenkorn, art books of all kinds, and the archives of Crown Point Press, the distinguished Bay Area printer of etchings. The AFGA also collects photography with depth on Bill Owens, Imogen Cunningham, and Eadweard Muybridge. Its first photos were Arnold Genthe's documentation of the immediate aftermath of the 1906 earthquake.

Something about the surroundings makes the European decorative arts stand tall next to the paintings, erasing the designation as something other than art. There's an octagonal Spanish ceiling from 1500 and a standout collection of Meissen porcelain.

Paired with all this classicism, the de Young, in Golden Gate Park, is another story altogether. Designed by Swiss architects Herzog & de Meuron after the 1989 Loma Prieta earthquake destroyed the old museum, it's a sharply angled, copper battleship with a twisted tower at its stern. The collection is strong on pre-Hispanic works from Teotihuacan and Peru, as well as Sub-Saharan Africa and Oceania. Its core collection focuses on American art from the 18th century on,

ranging from Native American to colonial to the Hudson River School (with Thomas Cole's *Prometheus Bound* and Frederic Edwin Church's *Rainy Season in the Tropics*.) The collection goes on into the 20th and 21st centuries, but prioritizes California work, including the Arts and Crafts movement, the Bay Area Figuratists, Funk, and the biggest collection of Japanese American artist Chiura Obata, including the stunning *Lake Basin in the High Sierra*. There's a group of 15 hanging sculptures by Ruth Asawa in the tower lobby—also the biggest collection of her work.

A recent acquisition of African American art provided by the Souls Grown Deep Foundation includes major pieces by Thornton Dial, Lonnie Holley, and Joe Minter.

OPPOSITE: AUGUSTE RODIN (ALEXIS RUDIER FONDEUR, MAKER), *THE THINKER*, 1904, CAST BRONZE, 72 x 38 x 54 IN. THE FINE ARTS MUSEUMS OF SAN FRANCISCO, GIFT OF ALMA DE BRETTEVILLE SPRECKELS, 1924.18.1

PHOTO: COURTESY THE FINE ARTS MUSEUMS OF SAN FRANCISCO

ABOVE: ANDY GOLDSWORTHY, *DRAWN STONE*, 2005, APPLETON GREENMOOR SANDSTONE, 19 x 1489 x 2157 IN. (HEIGHT OF TALLEST STONE, WIDTH OF ENTRY COURT, LENGTH OF CRACK). THE FINE ARTS MUSEUMS OF SAN FRANCISCO, MUSEUM PURCHASE, GIFT OF LONNA AND MARSHAL WAIS, 2004.5.

PHOTO: COURTESY THE FINE ARTS MUSEUMS OF SAN FRANCISCO

86

Asian Art Museum

200 LARKIN STREET
SAN FRANCISCO, CA 94102

Since it split off from the de Young Museum in Golden Gate Park, San Francisco's Asian Art Museum, housing one of the most comprehensive collections of Asian art in the country, lives in the upper floors of the Beaux-Arts civic center building that housed San Francisco Museum of Modern art (or SFMOMA; p. 217) for many years. Its 18,000 works cover all cultures in Asia, but it's known for its giant collection of exquisitely carved jade netsuke bottles from Japan. Among its masterpieces are a Zhou dynasty seated Buddha in bronze from the year 338 B.C., a rhinoceros-shaped vessel dating back to 1050 B.C., and sandstone figures of Shiva and Parvati from Cambodia. The museum delves deeper than most Asian art museums, devoting space to Himalayan art and to art from the Sikh kingdoms. It also has a completely reconstructed tea room from Kyoto on its second floor.

INSTALLATION VIEW OF THE JADE
TREASURY, ASIAN ART MUSEUM,
SAN FRANCISCO, CA.

PHOTO: COURTESY ASIAN ART MUSEUM
OF SAN FRANCISCO

87

San Francisco Museum of Modern Art

151 3RD STREET
SAN FRANCISCO, CA 94103

This is one of those museums with a distinguished history that only came into its own in the 2010s. It had Clyfford Still's first ever museum show in 1938, and, later, Arshile Gorky's and Jackson Pollock's, but it didn't have a real home until it built its (somewhat awkward) Mario Botta building off Market Street in 1995. Major acquisitions began to follow, including work by René Magritte, Piet Mondrian, Jasper Johns, Mark Rothko, and Frank Stella. (One of the replicas of Duchamp's infamous urinal readymade *Fountain* is here.) But in 2009, Doris and Donald Fisher, the founders of the Gap, decided to lend their famous collection to SFMOMA, as it's known, for 100 years, a group that includes Richard Serra, Richard Diebenkorn, Chuck Close, Cy Twombly, and many more postwar giants. By 2016, an expansion of the museum by the architecture firm Snøhetta made it a truly world-class modern-art museum.

The galleries are a pleasure to visit—the way they intersect with the birchwood stairs energizes the experience. Highlights include one of Diebenkorn's best "Ocean Park Series" paintings, *The Nest* by Louise Bourgeois, paintings by Diego Rivera and Frida Kahlo, and a chapel-like room devoted to Agnes Martin's paintings. Downstairs in the lobby is one of Richard Serra's *Torqued Ellipses* to play in. Also in the entry hall are two 3-story-tall panels that hold huge murals commissioned from Julie Mehretu, called *HOWL, eon (I, II)*; it's an abstracted, erased, and scribbled history of the American West—her biggest work ever—and will be up until 2020. (Previous artists who filled this space for a few years at a time include Kerry James Marshall and Sol LeWitt.)

NEARBY: Across Market Street and on the other side of Union Square, you'll find a large round fountain built into the stairs of the Grand Hyatt. Its bronze surface is completely covered in playful, cartoonish relief sculptures of San Francisco life. That it was made by Ruth Asawa—famous for having developed her elegant hanging-fabric sculptures at Black Mountain College—is a surprise. The figures, cast from dough shaped by local children, seem more in tune with Bay Area Funk and underground comics.

PAGES 216–17: INSTALLATION VIEW OF JULIE MEHRETU, *HOWL, EON (I, II)*, 2017, AT SAN FRANCISCO MUSEUM OF MODERN ART. COMMISSIONED BY THE SAN FRANCISCO MUSEUM OF MODERN ART; COLLECTION SFMOMA, GIFT OF HELEN AND CHARLES SCHWAB. © JULIE MEHRETU.

PHOTO: MATTHEW MILLMAN PHOTOGRAPHY.

RIGHT: ANSELM KIEFER GALLERY AT SAN FRANCISCO MUSEUM OF MODERN ART, CA.

PHOTO: KATHERINE DU TIEL

Pier 24 Photography

PIER 24
THE EMBARCADERO
SAN FRANCISCO, CA 94105

A new institution with a new kind of baseline anchoring its collection, Pier 24 Photography's obsession with the '60s and '70s makes it kind of like the Dia:Beacon of photography. Opened by the Pilara Foundation in 2010, there are 2 touchstones that drive the collection, both game-changing photo shows from the past. The first is MoMA's *New Documents* show from 1967, which featured Diane Arbus, Lee Friedlander, and Garry Winogrand. The second is the *New Topographics* show that George Eastman House mounted in 1975, which included Robert Adams, Lewis Baltz, Stephen Shore, and Bernd and Hilla Becher, who all took deadpan looks at landscapes. Both shows contributed to the moment when the art world started to take photography seriously, and they influenced generations of photographers and conceptual artists.

Pier 24—a massive maritime building on a dock—is big enough to keep huge amounts of its collection on view at any given time. It has expanded beyond the core photographers that got the ball rolling, but there's some fun to be had thinking about which of the above 2 shows any photographer you see here connects to. Looking to the past, it might be Berenice Abbott or Walker Evans; looking forward, Alec Soth's gritty travels in meth country or Yasumasa Morimura's psychosexual dress up. Pier 24 puts on a giant show made up of its collection every year or so, and the best create a dialogue between new photographers and the earlier generation that teaches us about both.

Pier 24 is open by appointment only—but it's not hard to get one, and admission is free.

NEARBY: Just down the street is Claes Oldenburg and Coosje van Bruggen's *Cupid's Span*—a giant bow and arrow jammed into the earth. Across the street from all the piers, at Justin Herman Plaza, is Armand Vaillancourt's Brutalist fountain— a wonderful oddity that has improbably survived both earthquakes and developers. If you leave Pier 24 after sundown, look up: The Bay Bridge, heading East to Oakland, is lit up, thanks to an installation by Leo Villareal. LED lights seem to rain from the cables, eventually filling in the entire outline of the suspension bridge. It's the biggest piece of work by this LED-obsessed artist, who has permanent pieces at the National Gallery, Albright-Knox, and the Brooklyn Museum.

GARRY WINOGRAND, *WOMEN ARE BEAUTIFUL*, 1957–73, DETAIL OF INSTALLATION VIEW, *THE GRAIN OF THE PRESENT*, PIER 24 PHOTOGRAPHY, SAN FRANCISCO, CA.

PHOTO: COURTESY PIER 24 PHOTOGRAPHY, SAN FRANCISCO

David Ireland House / 500 Capp Street Foundation

500 CAPP STREET
SAN FRANCISCO, CA 94110

This modest but sweet Italianate house on a side street in San Francisco's Mission District loomed large as a major art-world hub in the 1970s and 1980s. Its owner, David Ireland, set out in 1975 to clean out the house and make it his studio, but in the process of doing things like stripping out rotten windowsills, gathering up the 16 brooms he found on the premises, and attempting to remove a large safe that proceeded to tumble down the stairs, he began to see the house and his activities there as their own art piece. He also decided to live there.

Ireland's artwork involves everyday detritus and things that are even more ephemeral: light and space and sound. He was called "the most influential conceptual artist you've never heard of" by Jock Reynolds, formerly of the Yale University Art Gallery, and his work can be partly understood as one part Arte Povera (with its urge to make everyday objects meaningful) and one part Fluxus (with its disregard for boundaries between the arts, and disdain for the creation of artistic product). His greatest influences were Marcel Duchamp and Zen Buddhism.

The walls are key to Capp Street: Ireland sanded off all paint and then coated them with so many layers of polyurethane they look like saffron-colored glass. Scrapes and scratches—whether or not from Ireland's earlier adventures in home improvement—become frozen moments in time. The sheen captures surprising reflections as a visitor moves around the house, and Ireland's interventions in the architecture of

the space frame unexpected vistas or direct attention where he wants it.

He made sculptures out of stuff he found—most thrillingly, a kinetic sculpture called *Fire Drawing*, made from a pair of acetylene torches that serves as a chandelier in the upstairs parlor. Some things he kept as is, like the gold-leaf sign in the downstairs window that advertised the accordion-maker who preceded him. He lived in the space and hosted artist friends of all kinds until he had to move out a couple of years before his death in 2008.

In 2016, a major renovation was completed to preserve Ireland's own preservation of his eccentric demolition and to provide additional gallery space for over 3,000 of his artworks.

TWO INTERIOR VIEWS OF DAVID IRELAND HOUSE, SAN FRANCISCO, CA.

PHOTO: HENRIK KAM, COURTESY THE 500 CAPP STREET FOUNDATION

San Francisco Murals

VARIOUS LOCATIONS

The city has important murals in all corners—3 by Diego Rivera alone. Some of them are easy to see, some take a bit of finesse.

A. *ALLEGORY OF CALIFORNIA*, **DIEGO RIVERA** (155 SANSOME STREET). At the City Club downtown, Rivera completed his first fresco in the United States on the stairs to the dining room in 1931. Its main figure is Califia, a woman holding the bounty of the state's agriculture. The mural unspools across the ceiling with nude figures floating among airplanes—aeronautics being an up-and-coming industry at the time. There are tours on the first and third Monday of each month at 3 o'clock. Though it's a private club, you can also see the mural if you come to the pricey public brunch on Sunday.

B. *THE MAKING OF A FRESCO SHOWING THE BUILD-ING OF A CITY*, **DIEGO RIVERA** (800 CHESTNUT STREET). In another stairway, this time at the San Francisco Art Institute, Rivera created a self-referential trompe l'oeil masterpiece. In 2 layers, the fresco shows a partially completed scene of architectural and engineering triumphs as the city rises, and the wooden scaffolding and life-size team of workers creating the mural. Dead center, directing the work, is Rivera—with his butt pointed at the viewer. It's pretty funny. Viewable easily, daily.

C. *PAN AMERICAN UNITY*, **DIEGO RIVERA** (50 PHELAN AVENUE). At 75 feet long, Rivera's biggest fresco ever. Not all of the 10-panel piece fits in its home in the theater at City College out on the edge of town. Fresh off his Rockefeller Center dustup (in which he faced down demands to paint out Joseph Stalin and wound up getting painted over, see p. 58), Rivera seemed determined to pack everything in, including Abraham Lincoln; his wife, Frida Kahlo; Hitler; Mussolini; Charlie Chaplin; and Edward G. Robinson. The school is working on a dedicated building to properly display the mural, but for now it's still free to see—just call ahead because they're understaffed.

D. **THE RINCON CENTER MURALS, ANTON REFREGIER** (121 SPEAR STREET). In the Art Deco building that used to be the main post office (and is now a kind of mall and food court), a set of 27 murals explain the history of San Francisco. Refregier, perhaps inspired by Rivera's ambitousness in New York, attempted to pack social criticism into his history; for instance, in his original version, the monks at the mission were clearly well fed, while the Native Americans they bossed around looked gaunt and miserable. He lost 100 of these battles before the work was completed in 1948, and because he was Russian, he faced continued scrutiny in the McCarthy era. The style is kind of midcentury Mannerist Social Realism—stylized figures with elongated necks and sharp angles. The murals can be viewed daily for free, and the San Francisco Public Library offers occasional tours.

E. **THE COIT TOWER MURALS, WPA PROJECT** (1 TELE-GRAPH HILL). Around the base of the 1933 tower, thought to resemble a firehose, are murals showing life in San Francisco in the 1920s and '30s. There's some cheeky stuff the artists slipped in, some of which stirred up controversy, but its vibrant, complicated street scenes of life-size people are compelling. You can walk around the murals without paying the fee to go to the top.

F. **THE MISSION DISTRICT** (MISSION BOULEVARD AND 16TH STREET). San Francisco's historically Mexican Mission District features hundreds of murals, some wrapping around entire buildings. There's a neo-Mayan aesthetic here and plenty of Rivera influence, as well as some of Jose Clemente Orozco's darker sides. It all mixes with hip-hop street art and low-rider-culture imagery.

COIT TOWER MURALS, SAN FRANCISCO, CA.

PHOTO: CAROL M. HIGHSMITH ARCHIVE, LIBRARY OF CONGRESS, PRINTS AND PHOTOGRAPHS DIVISION

Oakland Museum of California

1000 OAK STREET
OAKLAND, CA 94607

**BERKELEY ART MUSEUM
AND PACIFIC FILM ARCHIVE**
2155 CENTER STREET
BERKELEY, CA 94720

This Brutalist bunker hides a mysteriously delightful sculpture garden and one of the first collections devoted entirely to California art from Carleton Watkins's photos of shipwrecks on Half Moon Bay to Mel Ramos's nude on California's state symbol—the brown bear. Built in 1969, it was the first major commission of architect Kevin Roche, who would go on to design the Ford Foundation in New York City and many expansions of the Metropolitan Museum of Art, including the gallery surrounding the Temple of Dendur (p. 49).

The concrete boxes that form the museum structure hold "rooms" of the garden, designed by America's top contemporary landscape architect Dan Kiley, creating a maze-like adventure on many levels. Sculptures in the garden include Mark di Suvero's *Homage to Charlie Parker*; and Viola Frey's *Man Observing*. The venerable architecture critic Ada Louise Huxtable said when it opened, "In terms of design and environment the Oakland Museum may be one of the most thoughtfully revolutionary structures in the world."

The whole museum is devoted to California, and it is, perhaps, the best regional museum of its kind in the country. The History wing includes elaborate dioramas from Native American villages to a Gold Rush–era bank to a beatnik's apartment, as if in dialogue with the more expected mountain lion and California condor dioramas in the Natural History wing. The Fine Art wing loses the chronological format by breaking Golden State art into themes: California land, California people, and California creativity. Within these, the curators create mash-ups that cross time and medium, and invite new takes.

The museum also celebrates the East Bay's own "Society of Six," a group of painters from the 1920s who pushed the boundaries of the very academic-oriented plein air painting of the region, and objects from the Bay Area's Arts and Crafts movement pioneers, Arthur and Lucia Mathews. Its paintings include prime works by Bay Area Figurative School painters like Wayne Thiebaud and David Park, as well as some of Richard Diebenkorn's best work. The sense of fun and funk in the Bay Area is also on display with a broad range of ceramic artists, such as Frey and Robert Arneson, and paintings by Jay DeFeo. Roche's pockmarked concrete sews all the museum's disparate elements together, inside and out.

One amazing and underrated piece is *The Planet* by J. B. Blunk, a circular structure in the museum's lobby, 19 feet in diameter and carved from a single redwood burl by the Marin County sculptor for the opening of the museum in 1969. Because it can be sat on, played on, spilled on, and climbed on—and has become such an icon of the museum—its perfection as a representative piece of California art is easy to overlook.

The Berkeley Art Museum opened in 1970 in another Brutalist masterpiece—this one all cantilevers that, sadly, finally caused the building to have to be retired after the 1987 earthquake. It had been founded on a gift of 45 paintings and a quarter million dollars from Hans Hofmann, and that collection remained on view for many years. The rest of the eclectic collection includes Albert Bierstadt, Joan Brown, Robert Colescott, Paul Gauguin, Ant Farm, Helen Frankenthaler, and artists related to the Fluxus movement. A new building was opened in 2016—a treatment of a 1939 Art Deco printing plant by architects Diller Scofidio + Renfro. The handsome building has lively public spaces and a theater, but much less room for the permanent collection. The adjacent Pacific Film Archive was founded in 1966 and is one of the most important homes for international film in the country.

ROOFTOP OF THE OAKLAND MUSEUM OF CALIFORNIA, OAKLAND, CA.

PHOTO: TERRY LORANT, COURTESY OMCA

Creative Growth Art Center

355 24TH STREET
OAKLAND, CA 94612

A humble ex-auto repair shop with a mission to give developmentally disabled adults a creative outlet since 1974, Creative Growth in downtown Oakland became famous for providing Judith Scott, an artist who can't see, hear, or speak, a place to create her sculptures. The organization has become an inspiration for others like it around the world, and the artists it fosters have gone on to have shows at major galleries and museums around the world, from London's blue-chip gallery White Cube to the American Folk Art Museum in New York to the Collection de l'Art Brut in Lausanne, Switzerland.

Creative Growth was founded by Florence Ludins-Katz, an artist and educator, and her husband, Elias Katz, in reaction to California's mass closing of psychiatric facilities. The couple's primary focus was to nurture artists with Down syndrome and autism, but their goal was never to simply offer art therapy—their intention was always to foster the creation of art that was great on its own merits. "Even though a human being may be handicapped or disabled, this does not change his need to fulfill himself to the greatest of his capacity," they wrote in their memoir.

Lately, Creative Growth has become a cause célèbre, with projects involving Marc Jacobs, Cindy Sherman, David Byrne, Scarlett Johansson, and *Paper Magazine*. Its annual benefit fashion show, which raises tons of money, lights up social media with models wearing creations designed by the center's artists.

A visitor to the space would know none of this. The unpretentious workrooms carry a palpable sense of the joy of creation. Ceramics, wall hangings, paintings, and collages line the walls and shelves—some are for sale at very good prices—and the staff and creators are clearly loving what they do. Respectful visitors often interact with the artists and even work side-by-side with them on special open-house days twice a year.

STOREFRONT FACADE OF CREATIVE GROWTH ART CENTER, OAKLAND, CA.
PHOTO: BEN BLACKWELL

92

Cantor Arts Center

328 LOMITA DRIVE AT MUSEUM WAY
STANFORD, CA 94305

THE ANDERSON COLLECTION
314 LOMITA DRIVE
STANFORD, CA 94305

Two museums worthy of their own visits are just steps away from each other on the Stanford campus. The Cantor Center, as it's known locally, is an encyclopedic museum whose original gallery space, full of antiquities collected by Leland Stanford Jr., was destroyed in the San Francisco earthquake of 1906. It's still strong, especially on Sub-Saharan Africa, Oceania, and Indonesian work. The highlights of its Native American collections are baskets by the Yurok, Karuk, and Hupa peoples. The Cantor also has 26 of Richard Diebenkorn's notebooks, with some always on display; a micro-collection of work by Jacob Lawrence; and Elmer Bischoff's beautiful *Interior with Cityscape*.

But the main point of a visit to the Cantor is the Auguste Rodin collection—it's the biggest grouping outside of Paris, and it includes over 250 works. There's *The Thinker*, of course, but there's also a rare casting of *The Gates of Hell*. And *The Burghers of Calais* gets an unusual treatment: The wracked and sorrowful Burghers are scattered across a courtyard, instead of in a group.

The Anderson Collection, in a sleek, light-filled building by Ennead Architects, is a well-edited collection of mostly postwar art with first-rate items representing each movement and artist it covers. There's Jackson Pollock's *Lucifer*, early and late Willem de Kooning, and standout pieces by Joan Mitchell (*Before, Again IV*), Mark Rothko, and Clyfford Still. But it also treats some of the West Coast art movements as equals with their New York School contemporaries. The Bay Area Figurative School is strong here, with work by Richard Diebenkorn, David Park, Wayne Thiebaud, Paul Wonner, Manuel Neri, Nathan Oliveira, and others. The California Light and Space artists show up with Robert Irwin, Larry Bell, and Billy Al Bengston. And even Funk, a San Francisco-based movement that doesn't get a lot of play in other art centers, gets its due with pieces by Roy De Forest, William T. Wiley, and Robert Arneson. Contemporary work manages to feel at home here, with Jennifer Bartlett, Susan Rothenberg, Elizabeth Murray, and Donald Sultan fitting right in. It's not huge—it's a perfect hour or so of enjoying the collection's juxtapositions.

NEARBY: The campus has sculptures of all kinds immersed in its plazas and paths, including large pieces by Kenneth Snelson, Andy Goldsworthy, and Alexander Calder. It has the *Stanford Wall* by Josef Albers—an imposing mass with subtle, ever-changing plays of light rippling across its bricks. Lee Kelly's *Stainless Garden* is sweet in its evocation of temple ruins, and Bay Area artist J. B. Blunk has a field full of stones he gathered in Marin—a warm and friendly version of Carl Andre's controversial *Stone Field Sculpture* in Connecticut.

INSTALLATION VIEW OF SELECTED WORKS BY KENNETH NOLAND, ROBERT MOTHERWELL, MARY WEATHERFORD, AND GABRIEL KOHN AT THE ANDERSON COLLECTION, STANFORD, CA.

PHOTO: ANDERSON TRUONG

93

Wildcat Hill, the Edward Weston Studio

251 HIGHWAY 1
CARMEL, CA 93923

One of America's first photographic masters, Edward Weston, was not the product of the photography world in New York City; born outside of Chicago and given his little Kodak box camera at age 16, he honed his skills at a commercial photo studio in what is now Glendale, California. His reputation grew enough around Southern California to land Mexican photographer Tina Modotti as a model—and a lover—and soon his nudes were world famous. He wound up at Wildcat Hill much later, partly because—despite his success with breakthrough shows at San Francisco's Legion of Honor, features in influential journals like *Photo Era*, and founding the influential Group f/64 with photographers Willard Van Dyke and Ansel Adams—it was still hard to make a buck with a camera.

His most famous nudes were of his second wife, Charis Wilson, on sand dunes around Santa Monica, and of close-up "portraits" of nautilus shells that give off a powerful erotic energy, so it was natural for him to stick to the beach when he moved to a plot of land owned by Charis's father. It's near Point Lobos, one of the greatest tide-pool zones in the state, and a beach that was named for him after his death.

Now his grandson Kim, also a photographer, tends to the studio just as it was left. It's also the Edward Weston headquarters, where prints are made from the original negatives and shown and sold—the only complete set is at the University of California at Santa Cruz, an hour north—but Kim and his wife, Gina, will pull them out to show you here, along with work from other Westons in the family (including Edward's son Brett

who was an accomplished abstract photographer). You're welcome to stay over—there's a bed-and-breakfast called the Bodie House on the property—and the guest book spanning the history back to 1947 is nothing short of awesome: Dorothea Lange, Robinson Jeffers, Allen Ginsberg, Gregory Corso, and more.

NEARBY: Mission Carmel (3080 Rio Road, Carmel-by-the-Sea), 8 miles away, is thought to be one of the most authentically restored of the California missions. Though their legacy is being rightfully rethought, the buildings dating back to 1770, and the Spanish antiques and artwork in them, are worthy of consideration. This mission also happens to be where Father Junipero Serra is interned. Though Serra was long treated as a hero in California history, monuments to him have more recently become lightning rods for protest across the state. The memorial to him here—the Father Serra cenotaph—shows him laid out on a slab, his successor saying goodbye. It's a Rodin-like bronze that was created in 1924 by California sculptor Jo Mora (an interesting character who lived with the Hopi, drew cartoons for Boston newspapers, studied with William Merritt Chase in New York, wrote books, worked as a cowboy, and eventually ran a gallery in Carmel).

J. Paul Getty Museum

1200 GETTY CENTER DRIVE
LOS ANGELES, CA 90049

THE GETTY VILLA
17985 PACIFIC COAST HIGHWAY
PACIFIC PALISADES, CA 90272

The world's wealthiest art institution isn't going to have just 1 hillside fortress with panoramic views on some of the most expensive real estate in the country—of course it has 2. The J. Paul Getty Trust runs both the Getty Villa, overlooking the Pacific Coast Highway, and its museum above the Sepulveda Pass and the 405 Highway.

There's a key moment when a visitor arrives at the Getty Museum that changes everything, and it happens in the garage. The moment you lock your car—which in Los Angeles is a second home and security blanket—and head toward the train up the hill, you give yourself over to art for the day in a way that few museums inspire. The 3-car train proceeds at a stately pace to the museum's perch above Los Angeles, and passengers spread out among the serene white plazas, stairs, and reflecting pools of an elaborate campus devoted to the researching, preserving, studying, and displaying of art.

Vincent van Gogh's magnificent *Irises* is here, and so are Peter Paul Rubens's *The Entombment* and Rembrandt's *The Abduction of Europa*—each worth a trip in their own right.

But what a visit to the Getty is really about is being a flaneur in a kind of utopian art city of your dreams. Getty Foundation buildings flank the museum buildings, and weekday visitors get a glimpse of serious work going on by scholars and archivists. The sense that the care for great art of the past is everyone's purpose is palpable on the walkways between buildings. There's a feeling that the more bunker-like buildings by Richard Meier, who designed the entire site, hold true treasure—and they do: The collection houses tens of thousands of priceless objects with must-see paintings, including Paul Gauguin's *Arii Matamoe* and Pontormo's *Portrait of a Halberdier* and Rembrandt's self-portrait *Rembrandt Laughing*. The collection and scholarship fuel temporary shows that always deliver some surprising angle on whole eras of work we think we already know, such as Buddhist art on China's Silk Road.

The garden would merit a place on this list even without the museum. The California artist from the 1960s Light and Space movement Robert Irwin—known for installation and public works that even *he* says are most successful when viewers don't realize he did anything at all—spent 5 years laying out terraces and paths and streams that cascade toward the city and the ocean from the main plazas above. He collaborated with master gardener Michael DeHart to plant native species in patterns and layouts that would constantly evolve over time. What's it all about? "He's asking you to simply attend," says Lawrence Weschler, who wrote a book about the garden. "That

is a profoundly philosophical posture toward the world. Stop and look at what's going on here!"

Forty minutes away from the museum is a whole other kind of experience, but also one where the setting and architecture are inextricable. J. Paul Getty, the very model of an early 20th-century industrialist, was crazy for Greek, Roman, and Etruscan antiquities, and when his personal gallery overflowed, he set out to build a proper museum down the hill from his house above the beach in Pacific Palisades. The resulting museum, modeled after the Villa of the Papyri at Herculaneum, opened in 1974. Along with major additions and renovations completed in the 1990s, all of the buildings and gardens are Roman-inspired. It's a perfect setting to reflect on some of the most important works in Western art, such as the *Lansdowne Herakles* from the year 125, which came from Hadrian's Villa outside Rome, and the spectacular *Marbury Hall Zeus*. Beyond the serene gardens with their colonnades, an authentic Greek amphitheater puts on Greek tragedies and comedies.

It's possible to see both Gettys in one day—and ticket prices encourage this—but the hard part is choosing which location to do last: Experiencing the sunset from either vista is unforgettable.

GETTY MUSEUM GARDEN DESIGNED
BY ROBERT IRWIN, LOS ANGELES, CA.
© ROBERT IRWIN.

PHOTO: JIM DUGGAN, © J. PAUL GETTY TRUST

Los Angeles County Museum of Art

5905 WILSHIRE BLVD
LOS ANGELES, CA 90036

An elaborate campus in the center of a sprawling metropolis, LACMA, as it's known, succeeds at being something for everyone like few other major institutions have. Greeting you as you pull up to the Wilshire Boulevard entrance, its *Urban Light* outdoor installation by native son Chris Burden is a must-Instagram attraction with a soul (it's made up of 202 streetlamps from the 1920s and '30s). LACMA's *Levitated Mass* by Michael Heizer, at 340 tons, is the largest example of Land Art in captivity. The museum has 2 permanent James Turrell installations, too, and houses one of the strongest collections of Californian modern and contemporary art anywhere, including Ed Kienholz's once-controversial 1964 *Back Seat Dodge '38*, and even Edward Ruscha's painting of the original museum building on fire.

LACMA also holds the largest collection of Latin American art in the United States. An eclectic Japanese pavilion was added to the original 1961 buildings in the 1980s, along with an Auguste Rodin sculpture garden. New additions given by billionaire philanthropist Eli Broad and designed by Renzo Piano opened around 2010. The move to adopt and commission monumental showstoppers like the Heizer and Burden have been driven by museum director Michael Govan, and the latest pavilion, dedicated to rotating exhibitions, was clearly influenced by his having been the head of the Dia Art Foundation, which is known for its impressive large-scale installations housed in a massive former factory building in Beacon, New York (p. 42).

The Broad Collection houses an extensive collection of postwar and contemporary artists such as Frank Stella, Jasper Johns, Jeff Koons, and Matthew Barney, all reached by a glass elevator whose shaft was designed by Barbara Kruger. The pre-Columbian collection boasts thousands of items from major burial sites such as Colima and Nayarit, and is housed in galleries designed by the artist Jorge Pardo that excite the imagination and upend expectations visitors have about engaging with dusty, ancient art.

The museum is a major cultural force in Los Angeles—with preservation projects involved with the Watts Towers (p. 243) and midcentury-modern houses by the likes of Richard Neutra, John Lautner, and Rudolf Schindler—and a robust film program that ties it to Hollywood. Visitors, too, can step across the street to visit the Petersen Automotive Museum (which itself strives to celebrate the automobile as an art form) and the energetic, scrappy Craft and Folk Art Museum.

CHRIS BURDEN, *URBAN LIGHT*, 2008, AT LOS ANGELES COUNTY MUSEUM OF ART, LOS ANGELES, CA.

PHOTO: © CHON KIT LEONG / 123RF.COM

96

Downtown Los Angeles

THE BROAD
221 S. GRAND AVENUE
LOS ANGELES, CA 90012

MOCA
250 S. GRAND AVENUE
LOS ANGELES, CA 90012

SIQUEIROS'S *AMÉRICA TROPICAL*
OLVERA STREET
845 N. ALAMEDA STREET
LOS ANGELES, CA 90012

For a city accused of having no center—even of having no soul—Los Angeles's downtown has become a newly vibrant place in the 21st century. With the opening of the international powerhouse gallery Hauser & Wirth's West Coast branch, and the newly renamed Institute of Contemporary Art's move from Santa Monica, there's actually art in the Arts District now. Two institutions anchor all of this—the Museum of Contemporary Art and the Broad Museum. MOCA is the granddaddy of the neighborhood, with its austere Arata Isozaki building housing its collection of major Abstract Expressionist works and its Minimalist and Post-Minimalist masters; with a crazily great Nancy Rubins object explosion out front called *Chas' Stainless Steel, Mark Thompson's Airplane Parts, About 1,000 Pounds of Stainless Steel Wire, and Gagosian's Beverly Hills Space at MOCA*; and with its rustic satellite—called the Geffen Contemporary, but still referred to fondly as the Temporary Contemporary—down the hill, pressed up against Little Tokyo.

Alongside its Pollocks and Rauschenbergs, MOCA has got some great Californians in its mix: Richard Diebenkorn, Ken Price, Sam Francis, John McLaughlin, Ed Moses, Paul McCarthy, Mike Kelley, and Doug Aitken. The Geffen was built from an old hardware-maker's building and architect Frank Gehry left it raw inside, with the original loading docks serving

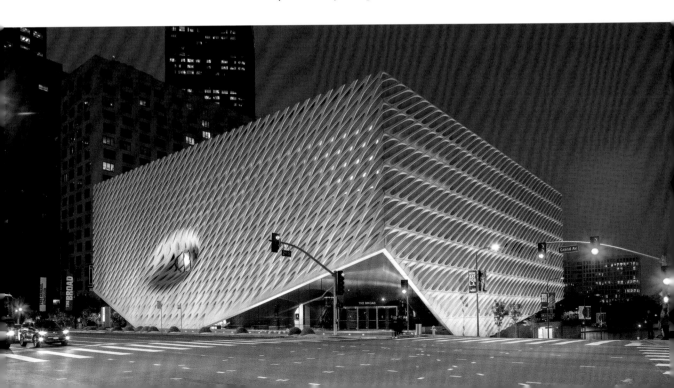

as its lobby. Between the 2 sites, it's the one Angelenos remember most fondly—it's been the site of some notorious shows, like Jeff Koons's premature 1980s retrospective, and then-director Jeffrey Deitch's controversial blockbuster devoted to street art.

The Broad was born when billionaire Eli Broad, who has his name on dozens of buildings around town, felt his collection needed more than his wing at LACMA (and his loans to museums all over the world) could offer. Next to the Walt Disney Concert Hall (a titanium-scaled swirl by Frank Gehry in Bilbao mode), Broad installed a Diller Scofidio + Renfro perforated cube and filled it with his collection devoted to the 1980s. It's got plenty of Koons of course, and the biggest

collection of Cindy Sherman photos anywhere. It's also got Jenny Holzer, Andy Warhol, Roy Lichtenstein, and Ed Ruscha. It has commissioned works, too, including a Julie Mehretu mural and a Yayoi Kusama *Infinity Mirrored Room*. Its restaurant, run by French Laundry alum Thomas Hollingsworth, features a mural and a less than appetizing formaldehyde sculpture by Damien Hirst.

The next stop downtown is both new and old: David Alfaro Siqueiros, the Mexican muralist who was one of the Big Three with Diego Rivera and José Clemente Orozco. (He's also credited with helping Jackson Pollock with his breakthrough drip technique while teaching in New York in the 1940s). Siqueiros's mural *América Tropical* was only recently restored in 2012 with

the help of the Getty Foundation, and placed in a dedicated space on Olvera Street, the quaint tourist trap meant to look like a Mexican town. Despite the commission being a celebration of the pursuit of happiness, he created a fresco depicting a Mayan temple taken over and destroyed by oppressive capitalist culture.

97

The Museum of Jurassic Technology

9341 VENICE BOULEVARD
CULVER CITY, CA 90232

Modeled after European *wunderkabinetts* in the Age of Enlightenment, this small building on busy Venice Boulevard manages to remain mysterious even 30 years after its founding. Its displays blur the lines between truth and lies, between things of value and trash, between scholarship and showmanship. It has all sprung from the imagination of David Wilson, a former filmmaker and CalArts graduate.

Visitors wander through a dark warren of displays a bit like visiting a haunted house, where they find a mixture of arcane religious objects, grotesque natural-history specimens, dubious relics, and the occasional more understandable entity (such as magician Ricky Jay's photographs of degraded cellulose nitrate dice, or the sculpture of John Paul II carved from a strand of human hair). Some pieces come with copious explanatory text, bewildering in its detail; some are displayed in a more shrine-like mode, such as the room devoted to the cosmonaut dogs of the Soviet Sputnik era.

It's better not to know too much before coming, or even think too much while here. Whatever it all is (collection of oddities, meta-museum, elaborate prank?), it inspires a sense

of wonder like almost no other museum. The whole creation was immortalized in Lawrence Weschler's book *Mr. Wilson's Cabinet of Wonder*, in which the author dives into every available rabbit hole opened by the Museum of Jurassic Technology.

One explanation for what's happening here came when, in 2001, Wilson was awarded a MacArthur Fellowship—the so-called genius grant. In its citation, the foundation wrote, "Wilson's work underscores the fragility of our beliefs, and at the same time, highlights the remarkable potential of the human imagination."

At the top of the building there's a small Moroccan-inspired aviary and free tea and cookies for visitors. Don't miss spending some time, phone put away, in this strange and charming oasis.

DIVINATION TABLE FROM THE EXHIBIT
THE WORLD IS BOUND WITH SECRET KNOTS: THE LIFE + WORK OF ATHANASIUS KIRCHER, 1602–1680, AT THE MUSEUM OF JURASSIC TECHNOLOGY, LOS ANGELES, CA.

98

Watts Towers

1727 EAST 107TH STREET
LOS ANGELES, CA 90002

Seventeen mysterious towers rose above the South Los Angeles working-class neighborhood of Watts between 1921 and 1954, all the work of an Italian-born tile mason named Simon Rodia. They're made of bent rebar wrapped in concrete and embedded with shards of ceramics and every other bit of broken junk imaginable. They were all improvised—there was no master plan—and the tallest tower reaches 99 feet. Though they resemble Antoni Gaudí's Barcelona masterpiece the Sagrada Familia from a distance, there's no known connection and no structural similarity. In fact, there's nothing like these towers in the world—they're one of only 9 folk art sites listed in the National Register of Historic Places. What it all means is unknown, but there's an immediate jolt a visitor gets from standing close to the spires while hearing about Rodia climbing them with only window-washer gear, and working his heart out for 30 years. It must be the same drive to build *up* that created Chichen Itza and Chartres and the Woolworth Building—only the Watts towers are condensed, and the signs of hard work make them more vital.

The story of how Rodia's towers were preserved is almost as gripping. The city of Los Angeles had hounded the artist over permits throughout his tenure on the towers, and soon after he gave up and moved away, they got serious about tearing them down. But a duo of Hollywood players and a group of artists and architects from around the world lobbied and arranged for a final showdown: Two cranes would do a stress test on the towers, the expectation being the whole thing would come crumbling down. But the cranes couldn't budge Rodia's work, despite the fact that nothing was anchored more than 2 feet deep in the ground. In fact, the test showed that Rodia's ingenious methods could be utilized in mainstream engineering projects. The towers were soon seen in architecture textbooks.

They then survived the decline of the neighborhood and the famous Watts riots, and soon became a symbol of pride for the now African American area. They show up in tons of pop-culture situations, from 1970s blaxploitation films to the TV show *The Simpsons*. The site eventually became a state park, and the Los Angeles County Museum of Art (p. 236), always interested in preserving local architectural wonders, helps maintain it.

The best way to see the Watts Towers is by tour, and 5 minutes in you realize you wouldn't have it any other way: The docents are the hardworking local minders of the Watts Tower Community Center—which provides opportunities in the arts to neighborhood residents—and they tell the story of Rodia so well, you'll be near tears by the end.

DETAIL OF WATTS TOWERS, LOS ANGELES, CA.

East of Los Angeles

While the city is pretty thin on art on its far west side (it's still mind-boggling that the unusual Museum of Jurassic Technology is the only non-Getty museum west of the 405 highway), cultural riches spill eastward right on into the desert. There are small museums devoted to Asian and contemporary art, and a bit farther out, a wonderful ceramics museum. But for our purposes here, these 2 lovely institutions stand out.

NORTON SIMON MUSEUM (411 WEST COLORADO BOULEVARD, PASADENA, CA 91105) This is a jewel box of a museum in the heart of Pasadena. Beloved by locals, the museum is just big enough to see everything in an hour or two. It's got terrific portraits by Frans Hals, Francisco de Goya, and Jean-Auguste-Dominique Ingres, and great examples of work by Rembrandt and Francisco de Zurbarán. There's a Giovanni Battista Tiepolo that's lit so well you might begin to value his ability to create weightlessness. The crowds are on the other end of the building where the Impressionist and Post-Impressionist work reigns. There's Edgar Degas, Claude Monet, Édouard Manet, and more. Plus Vincent van Gogh's *Portrait of a Peasant* and *Portrait of the Artist's Mother*, and a large beautiful painting by Édouard Vuillard. The modernist wing is the usual Francophile take on the subject, with everyone represented just a bit. The surprise is the last 2 rooms, where the collection turns local with heroes like Ed Moses, Sam Francis, John McLaughlin, and Larry Bell taking over the story. A pretty sculpture garden delivers Auguste Rodin, Jacques Lipchitz, David Smith, Berthe Morisot, and Beverly Pepper—all in bronze. By far the favorite of many regulars is a Nabis work you might miss until you exit—*Autumn: The Chestnut Gatherers* by Georges Lacombe.

HUNTINGTON LIBRARY (1151 OXFORD ROAD, SAN MARINO, CA 91108) This charming institution is known for its books (your Gutenberg Bibles and Shakespeare folios), its gardens, and its period rooms. It also puts on great art shows and has a permanent collection that is long

on *lonnnnng* paintings: the 18th-century British-portrait kind by Joshua Reynolds, George Romney, and, the big star here, Thomas Gainsborough. The Huntington has 7 of his most important works, including the most famous of all: his portrait of privilege known as *The Blue Boy* from 1779. The collection also includes work by Mary Cassatt, J. M. W. Turner, William Harnett, and a great painting by Walt Kuhn (the mostly forgotten painter who helped organize the Armory Show of 1913) called *Top Man*—a rustic kind of response to the full-bodied portraits by the Brits upstairs.

INSTALLATION VIEW OF TIEPOLO, *THE TRIUMPH OF VIRTUE AND NOBILITY OVER IGNORANCE*, C. 1740–50. NORTON SIMON MUSEUM, PASADENA, CA.

PHOTO: © NORTON SIMON ART FOUNDATION

99

A-Z West and Joshua Tree Outdoor Museum

JOSHUA TREE, CALIFORNIA

The high desert town of Joshua Tree is another place that has become a touchstone for artists deriving inspiration from the western landscape— its light, its openness, its danger. (See Taos and Marfa.) There's a rich history here, from ancient Pinto culture to more recent Native Americans and early settlers. It's also been a hideout for rock bands like America in the '70s and U2 in the '80s, which have added to its mystique. In addition, it's been home to artists such as Jack Pierson and the late Jason Rhoades, and a funky broken-down aesthetic that seems to infuse everything (and, thankfully, to resist cutesy artiness). There are 2 major places to visit— one seeks perfection in life, and though its objects are handcrafted, they're also futuristic; the other makes new work out of the trash of the past.

First is A-Z West, located on almost 70 acres right next to the national park where artist Andrea Zittel conducts experiments for living. Her work asks questions about how we live, and how our lives are dictated by social norms and values. Spread across the grounds are a Wagon Station encampment which consists of 12 science fiction-like inhabitable pods, a small shipping container compound, a "regenerating field," her own home full of prototypes for furniture, and a field of outdoor architecturally scaled sculptures called Planar Pavilions. A-Z West is also the site of Zittel's personal studio, which includes a weaving facility and ceramics area where bowls and textiles are produced and sold to support the overhead of the compound. (Bowls, or "A-Z West Containers," are the only dishes used for all eating and drinking functions at A-Z West.)

Tours are held once a month or so, and because this is the artist's personal residence, it must be stressed

that drop-ins are impossible. When no tours are available, you can visit the Planar Pavilions on the northern edge of the compound. You also can become a guinea pig for her by booking 1 week stays in 1 of 2 small Experimental Living Cabins—about 30 miles east— that have no power or water and are installed with abstracted forms for living called Planar Configurations. Zittel is also a founder of High Desert Test Sites, a local non-profit that supports works and programming by other artists throughout the year.

The next stop is the Outdoor Museum, the life work of Noah Purifoy. A graduate of the Chouinard Art Institute (the predecessor of CalArts), Purifoy made his first sculptural scrap pieces out of the wreckage of the Watts riots in 1965, for pieces in a show he organized with Judson Powell called *66 Signs of Neon*, which traveled all around California. (He was also a founder of the organization that saved Simon Rodia's Watts Towers, p. 243) Later, he bought land in Joshua Tree and didn't stop building until his death in 2004. The fantastical scrap works reward close-up looking, wandering, and taking in the long view. It's inventive technically, and evocative in its critique of modern culture. Purifoy grew up in Alabama, where he must have been influenced by the tradition of African American yard shows (see the last major remnant of this at Joe Minter's African Village outside of Birmingham, p. 157).

Over the hill from the Outdoor Museum is *Unagi*—a massive Land Art work made of salvaged train cars. Viewed from above, it's a bit like Peru's Nazca Lines, perhaps tracing the bodies of a tangle of eels. The museum is open daily, with occasional tours worth scheduling for.

OPPOSITE: ANDREA ZITTEL, WAGON STATION ENCAMPMENT AT A-Z WEST, JOSHUA TREE, CA.

PHOTO: LANCE BREWER, COURTESY THE ARTIST AND REGEN PROJECTS, LOS ANGELES

ABOVE: NOAH PURIFOY, *NO CONTEST*, 1991.

PHOTO: COURTESY NOAH PURIFOY FOUNDATION © 2018

100

Stuart Collection

UNIVERSITY OF CALIFORNIA,
SAN DIEGO
9500 GILMAN DRIVE
LA JOLLA, CA 92093

Sculpture parks tend to be contemplative places, on acreage away from the noise of day-to-day life. But this collection of site-specific conceptual work turns that all inside out. Deliberately integrated into the busy 35,000-student campus of UCSD, this art is being encountered and reacted to every minute of every day.

Visitors are given a treasure map of sorts, and you'll need to track down the works sprawled across the approximately 2,000-acre campus on foot. Some pieces are incorporated onto class buildings, such as John Baldessari's *READ/WRITE/THINK/DREAM*, featuring words, photographs, colored glass; or Bruce Nauman's *Vices and Virtues*, which involves 7-foot-high neon lights in the shape of words that alternate on the upper facade of a lab building; and Barbara Kruger's 2-story, clock-based pieces in the student-union atrium. Some sit in front of buildings and have become monuments carrying new meanings, such as Niki de Saint Phalle's crazy-looking *Sun God* (the first ever commission at the Stuart) and Tim Hawkinson's *Bear*—a teddy bear put together from Michael Heizer–worthy boulders. And some involve the trees skirting the edges of campus, such as Terry Allen's lead-encased eucalyptus trees that play music, or Robert Irwin's *Two Running Violet V Forms*—a fence raised off the ground and zig-zagging through a grove.

The most recent commission is unusual in that it's an art piece by the composer John Luther Adams: In another eucalyptus grove, Adams has arranged for music to be played based on the speed and intensity of wind blowing through at different heights and angles. The wind is real, and the wind is in charge. No one ever hears the same song twice.

But the showstopper on campus is always Do Ho Suh's *Fallen Star*, a small cottage that has improbably landed on the top edge of the School of Engineering—a precarious perch, to be sure. On the roof of the building that extends from the cottage is a fully grown garden and path, and the cottage itself is fully furnished, but its inside angles are discombobulating.

NEARBY: Niki de Saint Phalle has more work in the area—she moved to La Jolla after her husband, Jean Tinguely, died in 1991. In Kit Carson Park in Escondido (3333 Bear Valley Parkway) is the sculpture garden Queen Califia's Magical Circle. One of Saint Phalle's last major projects, it's named for the warrior queen of a mythical version of California. There are 9 large sculptures covered in symbols from pre-Columbian, Native American, and Mexican culture; a 400-foot-long, curving mosaic wall covered in ser-pents; and a maze. It's open Tuesday and Thursday mornings and the second Saturday of every month.

DO HO SUH, *FALLEN STAR*, 2012, ON THE CAMPUS OF UCSD, SAN DIEGO, CA.

PHOTO: PHILLIPE SCHOLZ RITTERMANN

101

Honolulu Museum of Art

900 SOUTH BERETANIA STREET
HONOLULU, HI 96814

DORIS DUKE'S SHANGRI LA
4055 PAPU CIRCLE
HONOLULU, HI 96816

This museum, spread out over 3 acres, would stand out in any state for its collection of American and European paintings old and new. But its importance is in its collection of Hawaiian art, both pre-colonial and post-, in the changing views of Hawaii in Western art along the way, and in its Asian collections—they include 10,000 Japanese woodblock prints donated by James A. Michener, with masterworks by Kitagawa Utamaro, Katsushika Hokusai, and the world's largest collection of Utagawa Hiroshige.

Anne Rice Cooke, a missionary's daughter born on Oahu in 1853, started the museum with her own collection in 1922, with a vision of building a flowing indoor/outdoor experience that was true to Hawaiian life, with courtyards punctuating the 32 galleries. Though it was designed by a New York architect, Bertram Goodhue, it influenced what became the Hawaiian-Modern style.

The Western painting galleries include a pretty extensive art-history seminar from the Renaissance to the Impressionists. American painting from John Singleton Copley and Charles Willson Peale to Thomas Eakins, John Singer Sargent, and Arthur Dove is all here. Postwar work from Helen Frankenthaler to Robert Motherwell to Philip Guston to Robert Rauschenberg is here, too. Sculpture checks in with Alexander Calder, Louise Nevelson, David Smith, Mark di Suvero, Isamu Noguchi, John McCracken, and, right out front, a kinetic George Rickey.

But the Hawaiian galleries are why you're here. They have incredible indigenous artworks, early views of the islands by Europeans dating back to 1788, Georgia O'Keeffe's views of Maui, and 20th-century work by artists born here. The regional modernist style that the building reflects shows up in the art by Marguerite Louis Blasingame, Isami Doi, Hon Chew Hee, Cornelia MacIntyre Foley, and Keichi Kimura. The native feather capes are the biggest showstoppers.

It was Cooke's idea to include all corners of Asia in the museum, and the museum has continued that mission with the most recently expanded galleries representing Korea and the Philippines. One of the highlights of the Asian collections is a Chinese figure of Guanyin in wood from the year 1025 whose casual pose seems as modern as anyone on the island today.

The museum also runs Spalding House—a former residence of Cooke's, where, in addition to a Japanese-inspired sculpture garden, an entire world by David Hockney is permanently installed.

Looking over legendary Diamond Head Beach, Doris Duke's Shangri La contains her collection of Islamic decorative art, mostly in the form of entire rooms transported from North Africa and Middle Eastern countries. Duke—the tobacco heiress known for philanthropy and gossip-column-worthy adventures—got respect in the islands by being the first non-Hawaiian woman to learn surfing (directly from Duke Kahanamoku, no less). She started Shangri La in 1937—some of it inspired by trips to places like the Taj Mahal on her honeymoon with James Cromwell—and continued to add to it as she traveled. Highlights include the Damascus Room with its extensive wood paneling in the Ottoman-Syrian style; the Syrian room which re-creates an entry hall from the 1500s; and collections in every material from glass to metal to textiles. Tilework is astounding throughout the complex, with examples dating back to 1260. The range of Ilkhanid tiles from Iran traces the arc of secular and religious Islamic art and innovations in glazes and techniques. All of this is laid out as Duke lived in it—like a time-traveling palace.

OPPOSITE: INSTALLATION VIEW OF THE AMERICAN GALLERY, HONOLULU MUSEUM OF ART, HONOLULU, HI.

PHOTO: SHUZO YEMOTO, COURTESY HONOLULU MUSEUM OF ART.

PAGES 252–53: INTERIOR AND EXTERIOR VIEWS OF SHANGRI LA, HONOLULU, HI. COURTESY SHANGRI LA HISTORICAL ARCHIVES, DORIS DUKE FOUNDATION FOR ISLAMIC ART, HONOLULU, HAWAI'I

PHOTO: TIM PORTER / OTTO

Suggested Itineraries

New England Itinerary

7 DAYS (LEAVING FROM BOSTON)

A jam-packed week with 10 museums, 5 historic artists' studios, and views that inspired some of America's best painters

DAY 1: In Boston, go to the **Isabella Stewart Gardner Museum** and the **Museum of Fine Arts**. Be sure to see Winslow Homer's *The Fog Warning* and *Driftwood* at the latter. Go visit Augustus Saint-Gaudens's **Robert Gould Shaw Memorial**, with its depiction of African American volunteer soldiers marching off to the Civil War, in Boston Common.

DAY 2: In the morning, head on I-95 all the way to the **Colby College Museum of Art** in Waterville, Maine, about 3 hours. Here you'll see the new Alex Katz wing, which includes lots of his Maine paintings, and work by Marsden Hartley, John Marin, and Terry Winters. Head over to any nice town in the Southern Penobscot Bay to stay the night.

DAY 3: In the morning, visit the **Farnsworth Art Museum** in Rockland and the **Olson House** in Cushing (yes—have your picture taken posed as Christina Olson crawling up the hill). Then check out the **Langlais Sculpture Preserve** nearby. An hour and a half down Highway 1 is Portland, where you can tour the **Winslow Homer Studio**, situated along the coast he painted many times late in life, and see works by more great Maine painters at the **Portland Museum of Art**.

DAY 4: Lots of driving, but worth it: take I-95 back down to Portsmouth, New Hampshire, and cut over to Dartmouth College (about 2 and a half hours) to see the José Clemente Orozco murals at the **Hood Museum of Art** (the rest of which is closed for renovation until late 2019). Then it's a quick jump down to the **Saint-Gaudens National Historic Site**—the artist's home and studio, run by the National Park Service—where you can see the original maquette for the Shaw Memorial, as well as a cast of the haunting Adams Memorial. Head down to Stockbridge, Massachusetts, and plan to stay a couple nights in the Berkshires.

DAYS 5 AND 6: You'll be busy. The **Clark Art Institute** is the star of the museums in the area, and **Chesterwood**, the summer home and studio of Saint-Gaudens's rival, Daniel Chester French, is a grand mansion and studio in Stockbridge that's not to be missed. (French designed the Lincoln Memorial here and its maquette is on display.) Nearby is the **Norman Rockwell Museum**, devoted to illustration, which also includes his **home and studio**, and the curiosity of **Frelinghuysen Morris House and Studio**, a Bauhaus-style dwelling for a couple of bon vivant arts patrons devoted to French modernism.

DAY 7: Cross back to Boston (take a bathroom break at the **Smith College Museum of Art**, where the restrooms are site-specific works by Ellen Driscoll and Sandy Skoglund) and finish the week at the **Harvard Art Museums**.

Hudson River Valley Itinerary

2 DAYS, 1 NIGHT (LEAVING FROM NEW YORK CITY)

A quick weekend trip through historic homes and aggressively Post-Minimalist art

DAY 1: Start at **The Met Cloisters** in upper Manhattan and take in the famous Unicorn Tapestries and views of the Hudson River. Cross the river at Tappan Zee Bridge and go to the **Edward Hopper House** in Nyack, New York. See the storefronts in town that were featured in his paintings, and pick up food for a picnic lunch. Head north up Route 9W to Haverstraw and keep an eye out for the house Hopper painted for *House by the Railroad* (which became the inspiration for the house in Alfred Hitchcock's *Psycho*, too). Keep going to **Storm King Art Center** near Cornwall. You'll want to

spend a couple hours here—and eat your lunch. Continue north and cross the Rip Van Winkle Bridge. Stay in Hudson for the night; check to see if there are any evening performance art events at **Basilica Hudson** near the railroad tracks.

DAY 2: Go to **Olana State Historic Site** outside Hudson and take a tour of the exotica-inspired home and studio of the most famous Hudson River School painter, Frederic Edwin Church. Then look at the galleries on Warren Street; the Carrie Haddad Gallery is a favorite. Take Route 22 out of town to the **Art Omi** sculpture park in Ghent and then follow it over to the Taconic Parkway. Head south to Beacon for a few hours at **Dia:Beacon**. After, stop by the **Magazzino Italian Art** center in Cold Spring for an Arte Povera experience with a view (you'll need to make an appointment) and then a quick look at the Chagall and Matisse windows commissioned by the Rockefellers for the **Union Church** of Pocantico Hills. Finally, as you head back into Manhattan on the east side, see if **Keith Haring's *Crack is Wack*** mural on a handball court near 125th Street is done being restored.

Southern Art Specialty Itinerary

9 DAYS (LEAVING FROM WASHINGTON, D.C.)

A real road trip through the Deep South. Start with a primer on masterpieces of Southern-made art in D.C. and then roll on down to see the art in its natural habitat

DAY 1: Visit the N**ational Museum of African American History and Culture** and the **Smithsonian American Art Museum**. Both have extraordinary collections of African American art; quite a bit from the south, including Gee's Bend quilts and work by Clementine Hunter. On view at the Smithsonian is a masterpiece of African American "yard show" art: James Hampton's *The Throne of the Third Heaven of the Nations' Millennium General Assembly*.

DAY 2: Go south about 2 hours to Richmond to visit the **Virginia Museum of Fine Arts**.

DAY 3: It's a long haul, about 5 hours, but if you time it for a Wednesday and make reservations, you can get a tour of the **Penland School of Crafts**, including its log cabin architecture, studios, and galleries (the galleries are open Tuesday through Sunday). Here, since 1923, weaving, ceramics, and work in other mediums has been taught (including by textile great Anni Albers). Spend the night in Asheville.

DAY 4: You'll want to call way ahead to the **Black Mountain College Museum and Arts Center** in Asheville to see if you can time your trip to any of the special events they hold at the original site of the legendary school that produced some of the most renowned creators in the postwar era. There's not a ton to see from the original site; it's a Christian boys' camp now, and not open to the public. The museum, which upgraded from a storefront to a stand-alone building in 2018, celebrates all the work that came out of that heady era—and holds weekly concerts and workshops. The **Asheville Art Museum** also collects the former artists of Black Mountain College.

DAY 5: It's a 4 hour haul to Summerville, Georgia, but once you arrive at **Howard Finster's Paradise Garden** you can stay put. Reserve the on-campus Airbnb unit for a one-of-a-kind folk art sleepover.

DAY 6: Head to Atlanta and plan to spend plenty of time at the huge **High Museum of Art**, which has one of the best collections of southern art anywhere and, thanks to the Souls Grown Deep Foundation, really important African American art from the south. There's great public art around town, but start with **Isamu Noguchi's** *Playscapes*, a playground—the only one the artist created—in Piedmont Park. Also in the park is contemporary African American artist **David Hammons's** *Free Nelson Mandela*, a sculpture tribute complete with jail cell bars. For more public art in the city: Harlem Renaissance star **Elizabeth Catlett** created a bronze relief sculpture at City Hall, and southern art comes into focus with **Thornton Dial's** tribute to Congressman John Lewis, which was made of found objects in Freedom Park.

DAY 7: It's a little more than 2 hours to Birmingham, Alabama, where on the outskirts of town you can stop by **Joe Minter's African Village in America**— often called the last of the great "yard shows," a constantly evolving display of upcycled scrap turned into sculpture with a message. Call ahead for a chance to meet Joe. The **Birmingham Museum of Art** surveys all of art history, and also has great works by Bill Traylor and Thornton Dial, textile art in the form of quilts, and work by other Alabama artists.

DAY 8: Start with a long 5 hour drive to the Mississippi Gulf Coast (stop in Montgomery to see Maya Lin's **Civil Rights Memorial** in front of the Southern Poverty Law Center). When you reach the coast, first visit the **Walter Anderson Museum of Art** in Ocean Springs, a tribute to the visionary nature artist who has been compared to Charles Burchfield. Across the bay is the **Ohr-O'Keefe Museum of Art**,

designed by Frank Gehry and dedicated to the "Mad Potter of Biloxi," George Ohr.

DAY 9: Take I-10 toward Baton Rouge, Louisiana, and visit **Melrose Plantation**, where Clementine Hunter learned to paint and left behind many murals. Finish the day with a drive to New Orleans and a visit at the **Ogden Museum of Southern Art**, the Smithsonian Institution's partner devoted entirely to southern art.

Rust Belt Itinerary

5 DAYS (LEAVING FROM DETROIT)

Temples to culture from the golden age of American industry and a few revolutionaries and visionaries.

DAY 1: You'll want a full day to spend at the **Detroit Institute of Arts** and its Diego Rivera murals. But make a quick trip to the **Heidelberg Project** to see how art responds—and uplifts—amid urban blight.

DAY 2: It's a little more than an hour to Toledo, where the **Toledo Museum of Art** celebrates the city's main product—glass. Its Glass Pavilion by Japanese architecture firm SANAA is a work of art in its own right. Another couple hours gets you to Cleveland, where there's another great encyclopedic museum from the Gilded Age with must-see paintings by Caravaggio, Picasso, and Turner. In Willard Park, next to City Hall, check out **Claes Oldenburg and Coosje van Bruggen's 50-foot-tall** *Free Stamp*.

DAY 3: Leave the Lake Eerie shore and drive 2 hours to Pittsburgh. Here, visit the **Andy Warhol Museum** (the basement Factory section is especially fun for kids),the **Carnegie Museum of Art**, and the rambunctious **Mattress Factory**.

DAY 4: Head north to Buffalo, New York, about 3 hours, to visit the **Albright-Knox Art Gallery**—a museum that has collected "contemporary art" since it was founded in the first years of the twentieth century. Across the street is the **Burchfield Penney Art Center**, a museum devoted to the visionary and hallucinatory work of underrated American painter Charles Burchfield.

DAY 5: Drive back across the north shore of Lake Eerie toward Detroit. If there's time, a worthy side trip is to the museum at the **Cranbrook Academy of Art** and the Art Deco masterpiece of a house designed by Eliel and Loja Saarinen, parents of Eero.

Texas Itinerary

4 DAYS (LEAVING FROM DALLAS)

A long weekend with some of the best-designed museums in the country and a couple of near-sacred modern art spaces

DAY 1: Start in Dallas, where you'll want to at least visit the **Kimbell Art Museum** and the **Nasher Sculpture Center**. Add the **Dallas Museum of Art** if you can.

DAY 2: Drive 3 and a half hours to Houston to see the **Menil Collection** (including its stand-alone Cy Twombly Gallery) and the **Rothko Chapel** (leave the phone in the car and don't rush this one—it rewards quiet contemplation). If you've got the stamina, the **Museum of Fine Arts** rounds out the day.

DAY 3: Get up before dawn and get over to Rice University to see **James Turrell's *Twilight Epiphany* Skyspace**. Sunset is a good time to go, too, but it gets mobbed—the sparser morning viewers make having your own epiphany more likely. Get breakfast and then make the 3 hour drive to Austin. Here you'll start with the **Blanton Museum of Art** and its chapel by Ellsworth Kelly, appropriately enough called *Austin*. Some have called it as powerful as Rothko's, though it is decidedly more upbeat. In the afternoon, get a map of the University of Texas campus and track down its extraordinary collection of public art. Out on the town in the evening, visit outsider artist and musician **Daniel Johnston's *Hi, How Are You* mural** at 21st and Guadalupe.

DAY 4: Visit the **Harry Ransom Center**, a research facility with rotating shows from its vast collection of cultural artifacts of all kinds (including illuminated manuscripts, writers' archives, movie storyboards, and a couple of Frida Kahlo paintings). Make the 3 hour drive back to Dallas in time to fit in the **Amon Carter Museum of American Art**.

Southwestern Itinerary

10 DAYS (LEAVING FROM LOS ANGELES)

A crazy adventure. Build the entire thing around stays at A-Z West in Joshua Tree and *The Lightning Field* in New Mexico if you can get them. Bring camping equipment and plenty of water.

DAY 1: Start in Los Angeles, where there's too much to see to include in this itinerary—but if you make one stop on the way out of town, make it the **Los Angeles County Museum of Art**, where you can take in Michael Heizer's *Levitated Mass* and Chris Burden's *Urban Light*—two undeniable monuments of the West—without even going inside. Head out of town into the desert about 3 hours toward Joshua Tree to visit the **Noah Purifoy Outdoor Desert Art Museum**. If you've made an appointment, make your visit to **Andrea Zittel's A-Z West**; it's a harder get, but it's possible to stay over in her experimental living pods for a real immersive experience.

DAY 2: Drive about 4 hours to Phoenix to experience the **Heard Museum**, known for both traditional and contemporary Native American arts. Just out of town is an unusual Skyspace, **James Turrell's *Air Apparent***, set in the middle of a rock garden by landscape architect Christy Ten Eyck and inspired by architecture of the region's ancient Hohokam people. Go in the evening, of course.

DAY 3: It's a long-haul day, but you can make it to Santa Fe in a little over 7 hours. Make it in time for the **Georgia O'Keeffe Museum** and double check your arrangements to visit her home and studio in Abiquiú for a look at **Ghost Ranch**, where she also once lived, and drive the countryside in search of vistas she made famous. The Girard Wing at the **Museum of International Folk Art** displays the fascinating collection of dolls and toys from all around the world by the prolific midcentury designer Alexander Girard.

DAYS 4 AND 5: Drive an hour north to Taos and set up a home base to explore the **Taos Pueblo** and the many small museums dedicated to the artists who have come and gone from the Taos art colony, including Agnes Martin, who has a chapel-like space complete with Donald Judd stools at the **Harwood Museum of Art**. Light and Space artist Larry Bell, who still works here, might let you take a tour of his studio.

DAY 6: If you've built your trip around a rare reservation to stay at **Walter De Maria's *The Lightning Field*** in northwestern New Mexico, do it now. If you're visiting the area after the year 2020, try to score a visit to **Charles Ross's** *Star Axis*, a piece of land art and architecture some forty years in the making. If not, head about 5 hours north to Denver. The big hit here is the **Clyfford Still Museum**, a brilliantly put together museum dedicated to the abstract expressionist most in tune with the west. The **Denver Art Museum** has one of the best collections of western and Native American art in the country.

DAY 7: Take a quick look at the **Kirkland Museum of Fine and Decorative Art**, which celebrates many lesser-known abstract painters from the region in a midcentury modern design setting. And then head west out of town in time to set up camp, weather permitting, in Utah's Sego Canyon.

DAY 8: Explore thousands of years of ancient rock art in **Sego Canyon** and nearby **Horseshoe Canyon**. The hikes are not difficult from the parking lots. Break camp and head north to Salt Lake City.

DAY 9: Go to the *Spiral Jetty*, Robert Smithson's land art masterpiece. Then eat, check your flashlights and water supply, and work your way around the lake to the ghost town of Lucin. Here, visit Nancy Holt's masterpiece *Sun Tunnels*. You'll want to be there at sunset to see the light transform the concrete cylinders and feel the connection to the night sky. Stay the night back in Salt Lake City.

DAY 10: Six hours on I-15, just before Las Vegas, you'll be able to visit **Michael Heizer's** *Double Negative*. In Las Vegas, there's some art to be seen at the **Shops at Crystals**, a luxury mall attached to a few hotels. Get a map and find the classic Frank Stella painting, the massive Nancy Rubins sculpture, and a throwaway James Turrell moment. If you're reading this after the year 2020, you may be able to visit Michael Heizer's epic lifework, *City*—perhaps the biggest art piece on earth. Get back to L.A. and get some rest.

First published in the United States of America in 2018 by

RIZZOLI ELECTA
A DIVISION OF RIZZOLI INTERNATIONAL PUBLICATIONS, INC.
300 PARK AVENUE SOUTH
NEW YORK, NY 10010
WWW.RIZZOLIUSA.COM

2018 2019 2020 2021 / 10 9 8 7 6 5 4 3 2 1
ISBN: 978-0-8478-6293-1
Library of Congress Control Number: 2018947930
Printed in China

Design by Kayleigh Jankowski

CHAPTER OPENER CREDITS

PAGES 10–11: METROPOLITAN MUSEUM OF ART, NEW YORK, NY
PHOTO: JOHN KELLERMAN/ALAMY STOCK PHOTO

PAGES 34–35: NATIONAL GALLERY OF ART, WASHINGTON, D.C.

PAGES 88–89: INSTALLATION VIEW, HIGH MUSEUM OF ART, ATLANTA, GA

PAGES 126–27: DETAIL OF GATEWAY ARCH, ST. LOUIS, MO
PHOTO: CAROL M. HIGHSMITH ARCHIVE, LIBRARY OF CONGRESS, PRINTS AND
PHOTOGRAPHS DIVISION

PAGES 150–51: SCULPTURES BY DONALD JUDD ON THE GROUNDS OF
    CHINATI FOUNDATION, MARFA, TX
PHOTO: THE LYDA HILL TEXAS COLLECTION OF PHOTOGRAPHS, CAROL M. HIGHSMITH
AMERICA PROJECT, LIBRARY OF CONGRESS, PRINTS AND PHOTOGRAPHS DIVISION

PAGES 182–83: DENVER ART MUSEUM, CO
PHOTO: FEDERICA GRASSI

PAGES 198–99: GEORGIA O'KEEFFE MUSEUM, SANTA FE, NM
PHOTO: ART RESOURCE, NY

PAGES 206–07: GETTY MUSEUM GARDEN DESIGNED BY ROBERT IRWIN.
    © ROBERT IRWIN
PHOTO: JIM DUGGAN, © J. PAUL GETTY TRUST